Algrove Publishing Limited
1090 Morrison Drive
Ottawa, Ontario
Canada K2H 1C2

Distributed in the United States by:
Veritas Tools Inc.
12 East River Street
Ogdensburg, New York 13669

Canadian Cataloguing in Publication Data

Main entry under title:
        Hundreds of things a girl can make : a hobby book for girls of all ages

2nd ed.
First ed. published Toronto : Musson Book Co., 1941-
Includes index.
ISBN 0-921335-35-0

        1. Handicraft. 2. Girls–Recreation.

TT171.H85 1998   745.5'0835'2   C98-900884-3

Printed in Canada

Publisher's Note

There are several things you should know about this reprint of the 1941 book of the same title. First, it is being published as a fundraiser for Ottawa's involvement in The Word On The Street, a free outdoor festival held every September in cities across Canada to celebrate reading and writing. Nationally, these festivals cooperate under the umbrella of a registered charity, yet each runs its own event, drawing upon writers, poets, artists, publishers and performers from the local area.

The festivals are non-profit, financed by exhibitor fees and sponsorship by organizations with a commitment to literacy for Canadians. We're pleased to help by donating to WOTS Ottawa 15 per cent of all revenues accruing to the publisher from this book.

Second, this book was published at the same time as a companion volume called *Hundreds of Things a Boy Can Make*. Not only was it then common to classify what was rightful male activity or rightful female activity (to the ultimate detriment of both, since the projects in the two books easily cross gender lines drawn by the most anachronistic among us), but it was still common to use cultural caricatures. In one or two places we have removed the most obnoxious of these.

Third, we would like to thank Musson Book Co. Ltd., Toronto, owners of the copyright in Canada, for graciously waiving royalty rights in favor of The Word On The Street.

As a final note, readers should remember that, with the minor exception noted above and the brief glossary added to clarify some terms, this is a faithful reprint of the 1941 edition and may recommend practices and procedures that are no longer considered advisable today.

Leonard G. Lee, Publisher
Ottawa
August, 1998

Hundreds of Things
A Girl Can Make

Hundreds of Things
A Girl Can Make

A HOBBY BOOK FOR GIRLS OF ALL AGES

TORONTO
THE MUSSON BOOK COMPANY LTD.
1 9 4 1

PREFACE

Most girls revel in making things when they know how. This is a book which will tell them how, in hundreds of cases. It is full of helpful suggestions and brilliant ideas. Not only are such matters as knitting, sewing, embroidering and crocheting dealt with clearly, but there are innumerable articles on making useful toys, while several of the more popular arts and crafts find a place among the pages.

Although the satisfaction of making things is sufficient in itself, it may be pointed out that a large number of the items included in this book will have an actual monetary value when carefully completed. Many of the articles, for instance, are admirable for selling at bazaars and similar functions. Thus the book has many uses and it is safe to say that its possessor will turn to it a thousand times for help and inspiration.

CONTENTS

Contents

8 Contents

Hundreds of Things a Girl Can Make

A HANDY KNITTING CASE

A case that will take wool, knitting needles, the article being knitted and, if desired, the printed directions of the pattern will prove extremely handy. This is how such a case may be made.

First, cut two pieces of thin wood, each 4½ by 3½ inches, and round off the corners. Then, take a sheet of tough, pliable card, 17 by 14

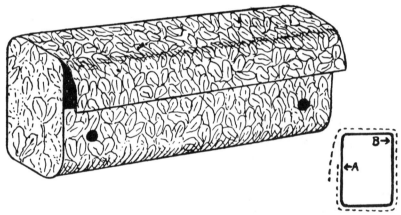

inches. Paste each face of the card in turn and stick a pretty piece of cretonne or fancy paper to cover both of them. Cover the two wooden ends in the same way. When dry, fasten the card to the edges of the wood with one inch panel pins and so form the case shown in the diagram. Begin nailing at A and finish at B (small sketch); then fold the card over the top edges and down the opposite side.

Slip an elastic band over the case to close the flap and, if desired, make two holes, shown black, through which the wool may be threaded while in use.

LINO PRINTING

This form of printing is very useful when it is desired to make several copies of a picture, such as when producing Christmas cards, book-plates and similar things.

The first step is to obtain a piece of thick linoleum, a trifle larger than the picture is to be. The surface should be gone over lightly with fine glass-paper to remove dirt, finger marks and inequalities in the surface; then the design is transferred to it by means of carbon-paper. It is not every design that suits lino printing. What is wanted is a picture that looks effective when reproduced in a solid colour, such as black, with the white paper to throw the black into relief. There can be, for instance, no half tones. The accompanying sketch is offered as a typical piece of work which will make these needs quite clear.

Having attended to the preliminaries, the cutting is begun. A sharp pocket-knife does very well for this, although special lino knives can be purchased. A line is cut all round the edge of the design. It should not be a vertical cut, but one that slopes away from the areas that are to print black. Then, when the outline has been made, the parts that are to print white are scooped out with a tiny gouge, a tool which can be bought for sixpence. It is advisable to arrange for a black line to run all round the picture to serve as a frame.

When the block is finished, the printing is taken in hand. Smear some thick ink, such as is used for cyclostyles, on the upstanding areas of the lino block and, then, press the block evenly in contact with a sheet of unglazed fairly thin paper. On lifting the paper, an impression of the picture should be the result. If it is not quite satisfactory, try pressing the paper in contact with the block, rubbing every part of it with a finger, and it is not a bad idea to use paper that is slightly damp.

Lino Printing

Novel Flower Bowls

NOVEL FLOWER BOWLS

Very useful flower bowls, suitable for growing bulbs and small root plants, are easily made from discarded gramophone records. Take the records and place them in boiling water for a short time. This makes them soft, when they can be moulded into any shape suitable for bowls. On cooling down, they will become quite hard again. Give them a coat of some bright coloured enamel, if thought desirable. The centre hole serves for drainage, but it can be closed by means of a cork, should this be considered necessary.

A TRIAL OF SKILL

Take an unused pencil or a piece of wood of much the same diameter and length : then get two light metal rings, about 1½ inches in diameter.

We have found curtain rings suitable for the purpose. Tie the rings to the mid-point of the pencil, as shown in the diagram.

The game is to hold the pencil in the middle and then to jerk one ring on to each end of the pencil. It is easy enough to get one ring on, but the tendency is to jerk it off while you are trying your utmost to put the other one in position. Just see what a lot of fun the rings can give you!

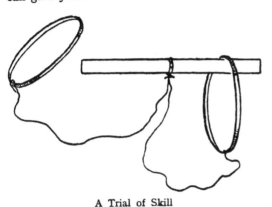

A Trial of Skill

A JOLLY BOOKMARK

Bookmarks are a necessity, if you read at all, and, of course, you do. Here is a jolly design, for one which you can easily make. Draw it on a postcard and colour it. Give the eyes a touch of green, make the lips red, shade the cheeks with brown and put on a gorgeous blue bow. Then cut out the shape, as shown, and the bookmark is finished. The two upright cuts, shown in the illustration, enable the bookmark to be clipped on any particular page desired.

A Jolly Bookmark

A FILE FOR KEEPING USEFUL INFORMATION

Purchase a packet of twenty-five large envelopes, all the same size. Pile them up with their openings all the same way and, then, print on the first a large letter A, a large B on the second, and so on through the alphabet, giving the last one the two letters, Y and Z.

Now, obtain a coil of adhesive paper or tape and cut several strips, each 3 inches long. Take envelopes A and B and stick two pieces of the tape on them to act as hinges. Place the tape on the front of A and the back of B. Do this both top and bottom, and do not bring the envelopes too close together, but leave $\frac{1}{16}$ inch between them.

Next, stick two more hinges on the back of C and thread them through the opening between A and B, then press them down on the front of B. After that continue, in the same way, with all the remaining envelopes.

Note that the hinges on A, C, E, G, etc., must come close to the ends of the envelopes, while B, D, F, H, etc., should be placed further inwards.

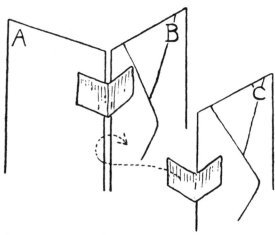

You now have a very useful alphabetic file, suitable for storing all sorts of information that you want to keep handy.

WAKING UP THE BUTTERFLIES

Get a thin sheet of typewriting paper and draw on it a few small butterflies or moths. Colour them and cut them out. Then glue to each a length of cotton, about 4 inches, and glue the free ends of the cotton to a sheet of stout paper. The diagram explains all this perfectly

Next, take a sheet of brown paper, put it in a hot oven for a few seconds and when nice and hot, rub it vigorously for a short while. Rub one way only. Immediately, hold the paper over the sheet with the butterflies lying on it: they will quickly come to life and begin to fly round. Repeat the experiment as often as you like.

A NEWSPAPER STAND

This newspaper stand will help to keep the living room tidy. It is not difficult to make, being constructed of three-ply. The dimensions should be about 18 inches long, 12 inches high and 5 inches deep.

Cut the necessary pieces of wood and smooth the edges ; then glue

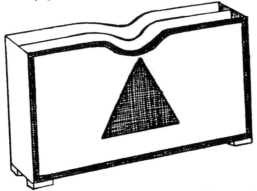

the joins and tack them with light panel pins. Fill any imperfect joins with plastic wood, give all the faces a good sand-papering and apply two or three coats of glossy paint. Ornament the front face in some modernistic way, as suggested.

If preferred, the stand can be made of thick millboard. Do not use panel pins for the joins then. Cover with artistic paper or cretonne.

LEAVES AND FRUIT BEARING YOUR INITIAL

Would you like to obtain some leaves and fruit bearing the first letter of your christian name ? Then obtain some thin black paper and cut out several examples of your initial. Take them into the garden and select a number of flat leaves and some well developed

apples, pears or other hard fruits. Stick one initial on each, choosing positions for them that face the sun. You must do this fairly early in the season, in the case of the fruits, before they have begun to colour, but leaves may be done at any time before the late summer.

When the autumn arrives, pick the leaves and fruit, wash off the paper initials and you will find that the letter is imprinted on each of them in a colour lighter than the surroundings.

A CIRCULAR CODE

There are various ways of making up a code, but here is an ingenious one. Cut two circles as shown in the sketch. Divide the circumference of both into twenty-six compartments and put a letter of the alphabet in each of them. Then, put the smaller circle centrally over the larger one and slip a pin through the centres, so that both will revolve freely.

Having done all this, make an exact duplicate of the circles, being very careful to see that the order of the letters on the smaller circles

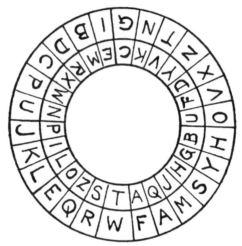

is exactly the same, also the order of the letters on the larger circles is exactly the same. Hand one of the gadgets to your friend and keep the other yourself.

All you have to do when you want to send her a coded message is to begin by stating, for example, *I*=*K*, which means that *I* on the inner circle stands for *K* on the outer circle. Then the real message as spelt out on the inner circle would be given in corresponding letters on the outer circle.

Of course, by rotating the circles, any inner letter may be brought into line with any outer letter to determine the key. Your friend decodes by setting her gadget and then transcribes your message from it.

A HINT ABOUT SHEET-MUSIC

Everyone who has played the piano must have experienced the difficulty of turning over a page of music whilst playing the notes. Not infrequently, the whole of the piece falls on to the key-board and you have to stop playing whilst the music is being put back in position.

To guard against all this, stick an ear of paper on each sheet that has to be turned over, so that it stands at least an inch beyond the edge of the page. Just before starting, turn up these ears slightly. Then, while you are playing, it is quite a simple matter to turn over quickly and without accidents.

Use gummed paper strips for the ears and stick them as shown in the right hand sketch. Note how the strip is folded back to provide extra strength. The strips should not be gummed in relatively the same position on each page, but all at different levels.

A STRING HOLDER

We have made dozens of this string holder for bazaars, and they have always sold readily. A base of wood about 2 by 3 inches is cut first, and then two upright sides are nailed to it. The diagram explains

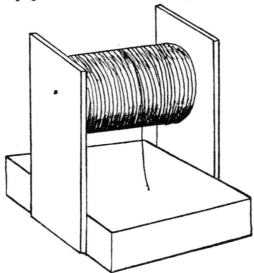

how this is done. Next, an empty reel is obtained or, if one cannot be procured, a stout piece of cylindrical rod is cut to the length of the opening between the two sides.

If a cotton or thread reel is used, it is held in position by a nail driven through each upright support into each end of the reel, the bore through the centre of the reel being large enough to permit its revolving on the nails. If a rod is used, first bore a hole in each of the uprights, two inches or so from the top, and central in the width, large enough for a nail to slip through easily as far as its head. Insert a nail through each of these holes and drive one into the centre of each end of the rod whilst it is held in position between the uprights.

A coat of quick-drying enamel, bright in colour, is applied and, when this has hardened, a gay tinted string is wound on to the reel. The cost is about 4d. if several are made, and they sell well at 1s. 6d.

PAPER CHAINS

Chains made of bright coloured tissue-paper have a very cheery appearance when rooms need decorating. They are easily made in the following way :

Take a sheet of tissue paper, 9 inches square, and fold it diagonally into four, thus obtaining a triangle like the one in the illustration. Then, make the cuts, as shown. Be careful to note that no cut reaches from one side to the other, and note, also, that they reach the sides alternately. Now open the sheet out flat and make a second one exactly like it, but of a different coloured paper.

Next, stick the two sheets together by giving them a dab of gum at the corners. Wait till the gum has dried and, then, draw out the paper by pulling gently at the centre. Pull one centre to the left and the other to the right and you have a nice long chain. Make half-a-dozen of these and you have sufficient to bedeck a whole room.

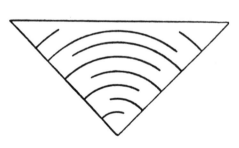

Paper Chains

An Initial Stamp

AN INITIAL STAMP

It is often useful to be able to stamp your things with your initial. To make such a stamp, cut a smooth slice off a raw potato and, then, shape the letter by trimming away the surrounding parts of the potato. Note that certain letters are not the same in reverse as they are when drawn direct and that for the purposes of a stamp they must be cut in reverse. Therefore, print the initial on a piece of paper and look at it in a mirror. Then, cut the stamp according to what you see in the mirror.

Use a rubber stamp pad for the ink or, if one is not handy, a tin of boot blacking is almost as good.

A GAY BOWL OF TULIPS

Here is a delightful show of tulips ! And they are all made out of wood and paint. What is more, they will last for a whole season and do not need renewing every few days.

Get some thin pieces of fretwood, borrow your brother's fretsaw and cut out the shapes, much as we have shown them. You will find it practicable to have a leaf attached to almost every flower. When the shapes are made, go round the edges with a fine piece of glass-paper and rub off any threads or jagged pieces of wood, but be careful you do not break the delicate stalks. Then, get three or four tins of cellulose

paints of different colours, including red, yellow and blue. With these, you can make green for the stalks by mixing yellow and blue. Purple can be obtained with blue and red, and orange with yellow and red.

Colour the flowers as you think fit, but first put on an " all-over " colour and, when it has dried, put in the detail lines with other colours. Aim at bright effects and do not trouble too much about making the flowers look absolutely natural.

Fill a bulb bowl with earth and a covering of moss ; then stick the flower shapes into the earth. If you have no bowls handy, a suitable tin will serve instead. Give it a coat of black stove enamel and it will form a pleasing contrast with the gay-coloured tulips.

A " MAKE-BELIEVE " WATER LILY

Take a well-shaped orange, having a fairly tough skin. With a pocket knife, make eight cuts from the top almost down to the bottom, but not quite. Now unpeel the skin, taking care not to break it. Lift

c

out the whole of the orange and you will have a beautiful lily-like flower. Trim the tips of the imitation petals with scissors if they are at all ragged. Then gather a few broad leaves from the garden—they should be fleshy ones—and pin them to the base of the imitation lily. Make them appear as natural as possible. Float the arrangement on a wide, shallow bowl, containing a little water.

HOME-MADE FLOWER VASES

Here is a good method of making attractive flower vases. Collect a few glass jam jars—ugly things in their way, it is true. Put them in an oven until they are quite hot. See that they are dry and that the heat has gone beyond the pitch of steaming them. Take them one by one and drop a large lump of red sealing wax in the first, blue sealing wax in the second, purple in the third, and so on. When the wax is quite melted, roll the jar about until the whole of the inside has a thick coating. If the wax grows cold before the colour has covered the whole surface, heat the jar a little more. When finished, the jar will look quite attractive.

It is not a bad plan to cover partially the inside of a jar with one colour; then use another, and again a third. If the jar is whirled round, while each colour is being applied, the final effect will be that of a rainbow.

A NEAT PUZZLE

On the left of the diagram is a shape something like the letter L. Cut it out of a piece of card and ask your friends if they can divide it into four pieces all the same size and same shape. They will not find it easy. For your own assistance, the right-hand diagram is given so that you will know how to do it yourself.

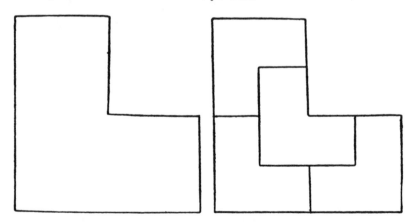

Why not cut out several pieces of the L and hand one to all your guests when you next have a party? It will be a jolly way to spend a few minutes, especially if you offer a small prize to the first solver.

DRAWING A SCROLL

It often happens when doing some piece of craft-work designing, that it is necessary to draw a scroll. With ordinary apparatus, this is a somewhat puzzling figure to construct, but here is a way that permits it to be done quite readily.

Get a stout needle and wind some cotton around it, close to the point. Then, tie the free end of the cotton around a pencil or pen. Stick the needle into the paper so that it is quite firm, place the pencil where the scroll is to begin and holding it quite upright, let the pencil follow the path which the cotton allows. As the pencil runs round the needle, the cotton is gradually unwound and this action forms the scroll.

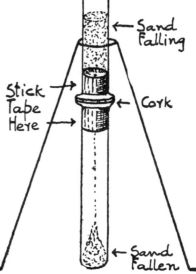

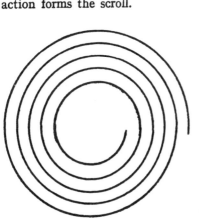

Drawing a Scroll

An Egg Timer

AN EGG TIMER

Take two test-tubes of the same size and get a cork that fits the mouth of them. Most corks taper at one end, but you need one that is as wide at the bottom as at the top. Bore a hole through the centre of it and countersink the two ends. You can do this easily with a brace and suitable bit, whilst the cork is held in a vice.

Now, procure some dry silver sand, sift it very carefully and put it into one of the tubes. Then, insert the cork half way and fit the other test-tube to the remaining half.

Turn the test-tube, containing sand, uppermost, and let the sand run through into the other test-tube for the exact length of time that eggs are usually boiled in your home, then pull off the top tube and shake out the surplus sand. The sand in the bottom tube is the correct amount for your conditions.

Refit the top test-tube, stick a strip of adhesive tape around the junction of the two tubes and make a wire tripod to stand it upright.

JAZZ-COLOURED FLOWER VASES

Some very delightful flower vases can be made from wide-mouthed bottles and glass jam jars in the following way :

First of all, you must provide yourself with three or four tins of cellulose paint of different colours, a tin of thinning mixture, a brush, and a supply of clean bottles or jars.

When about to commence operations, put an old glove on your left hand and push the hand inside one of the articles to be ornamented. If the mouth of the article is too constricted to permit of this, grip a stick about a foot long and turn the jar upside-down on it.

Holding a tin of paint in the right hand, pour about a tablespoonful of the contents on to the upturned base of the article, and let it run slowly down the sides. A twist of the wrist, now and again, will cause the paint to flow wherever you require it to go.

Wait a few moments, then pour on a second colour in the same way as you did the first, only direct the flow of paint in different directions. Follow with a third colour, and if you like, a fourth. By this time, the whole of the outer surface of the article will be covered and that is what you want.

At this stage, the glass will have a very pleasing appearance, but you can make it considerably more attractive by finishing off with a table-spoonful of the thinning mixture. When this is poured on, it helps to soften the paints, and, by twisting the jar or bottle smartly, you can make the paints run and cause an " all-over " mottled pattern.

Cellulose paints dry very rapidly and the vase can be put into use within an hour of being painted. Water has practically no effect on the paints, and the surface will last in good condition for a year, at least, when it can be coloured afresh.

A GARDEN IN A DISH

Have you ever thought how easy it is to make a miniature garden on a tray ? Some very fascinating effects can be obtained, with a little scheming. At the moment, we have a very flourishing garden of this kind.

Shall we describe how it was made ? First, we obtained a shallow baking dish about 18 inches long and a foot wide. The dish is made of a material that looks like the substance used for red flower-pots, but it is glazed on the inside. A tin tray would have been cheaper, but the dish keeps cooler in hot weather, and the growing plants do not droop so readily in it.

The next step was to spread some good leaf mould all over the bottom of the dish, making it an inch deep in the shallowest part. In some places it is considerably more than this, because we wanted to provide hills as well as dales. Then, a few stones were spread about, to resemble rocks. From the top of one rock to another, we fashioned a rustic bridge, and, in a corner of the dish, is a woodman's hut. There are two small ponds ; they are watch glasses, slightly sunk in the earth. If you cannot get such a glass, a large cockle shell will do equally well.

But what we wanted was to have a growing garden ; so, in the autumn, we found three or four acorns and planted them in the mould. At the moment, they are elegant trees, a foot high. There is a patch of grass which we keep neatly clipped, and, in the crevices of the rocks, are a few pads of moss. In several places, there are tiny rock plants which are thriving very well, some have even blossomed.

This garden in a dish is usually kept in the conservatory, and, of course, it has to be watered periodically. In this matter, the secret lies in supplying a little water often and not a great deal at long intervals. Evaporation will, then, keep the dish from becoming fouled and no drainage is necessary. With a little ingenuity, you ought to be able to make one that is every bit as attractive.

A FLOWER SUPPORT

A good many flowers, possessing long stalks, are apt to be troublesome when gathered and placed in vases, or when growing in pots. They lean over and look very untidy. The narcissus family provides a case in point.

A good way to overcome the difficulty is to make some ornamental supports. Take a pea-stick, as used in the garden, cut off a length of about ten inches and split the cane, length-wise, into two or three

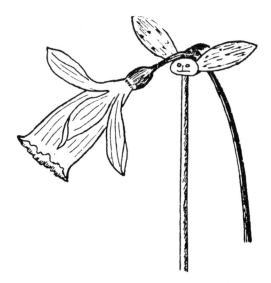

strips. Then, heat up some green sealing wax and place a good sized blob at the tip of each length. When the wax is slighly plastic, mould it with the fingers into the shape of the body of some winged creature and press in two thin pieces of wood to look like wings. The wood is not much thicker than a shaving and is thin enough to be trimmed to the required shape by means of scissors.

When the wax has hardened, paint the stick and the wings with some green ink, and then the support is finished.

You will see how to use it by looking at the diagram. The lolling stalk is held up by the body of the winged creature and the wings prevent it rolling out of position.

PAPER FLOWERS

Paper flowers enter into the decoration of so many articles that a few words on how to make them will probably be useful.

The requirements are a supply of crêpe paper of various colours and some fairly substantial wire. Instead of wire it often provides variety if selected pieces of twigs are used.

Since most flowers consist of a number of similar parts, as in the case of the petals, it generally shortens the work if the crêpe paper is folded and one cutting made to serve for many sections. Take, for instance, a flower such as a primrose. A piece of light yellow paper about 1½ inches square if folded into four and the edge scalloped to resemble the edge of the petal. (See A.) When the paper is spread out again, the shape

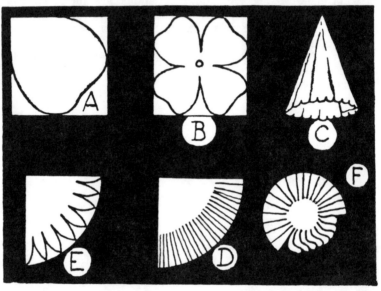

is a very faithful reproduction of the real blossom. (See B.) A few spots of brown paint may be dotted in the centre and the flower is completed, except for fixing it to the stalk. This is done by pinching the centre of the paper into the shape of a V and placing the point of the V beside a piece of wire and binding the two together by means of a thin strip of green paper. A touch of paste or gum at both ends of the strip holds it firmly in position.

Bell-shaped flowers, of which there are many, are made by folding the paper in four and cutting the edge into a quadrant ; then gripping the pointed tip, forcing a finger within the folds, and running it round in a circular motion. This opens it out somewhat ; but if the bell is not sufficiently formed the tip should be held by the left hand and the fingers of the right should stroke it to the required shape. (See C.) It should be noted that a bell requires a good-sized circle of paper—more than would be imagined at first.

Flowers with a multitude of petals, such as the common daisy or the ox-eyed daisy, are shaped by folding the paper into four, cutting the edge into a quadrant, and then running the scissors from the quadrant towards the centre a number of times. These cuts give the edge the requisite fringe of petals. (See D.) If the petals have a decided shape the fringe is cut as shown in Diagram E ; and if the petals are curled it is quite easy to impart the necessary twist by gripping the base of each against the edge of a pencil and running it up to the tip. (See F.) In the case of double flowers, the best way to make them is to cut two —or, better still, three—sections alike, but of different sizes, and to fit them one inside the other, the largest being outside.

When it is desired to provide a flower with stamens—those little hair-like threads at the centre—cut short lengths of sewing cotton, dip them in a very wet paste made of flower and water, and hang them up to dry tip downwards. On becoming dry it will be found that the paste has slightly run down them and formed little knobs at the tip. To fix them in position take four or five of the threads, each a little longer than desired, push them through a small hole made in the centre of the flower, and bind them to the stalk, as already explained.

There is no reason why touches of colour should not be added to the paper flowers, when, by so doing, they will be made to look more natural.

MAKING A COLLECTION OF WILD FLOWERS

Whilst it is not always possible to preserve wild flowers so that they retain all their natural beauties, it is a fact that a collection of pressed blossoms may be both a beautiful and an interesting possession.

We will suppose that the nature-lover has reached home with a varied assortment of flowers ; her first business will be to dry and press them ; the arranging and mounting will come later. Upon the drying, let it be said, will depend more than most amateur botanists imagine, for while there is moisture in the blossoms and leaves, the delicate colouring matter will continue to disappear ; but once the specimens are practically dry, the fading will be almost arrested. The point emerging from this statement is that the drying should be expedited with all haste, but not, of course, to the point of destroying the delicate textures.

The best way to dry a flower is to place it between several thick-nesses of white blotting-paper, and to apply gentle pressure, increasing it daily. Full pressure must not be applied at the start, because this only crushes. In a week or a fort-night the process will be finished.

The pressing calls for a certain amount of contriving. A big, heavy book makes a capital press for the early stages of the work, but, later, a trouser press or a linen press will do the work quicker and better. The book should not be of any value, as it is sure to be spoilt, but the trouser press is hardly the thing to begin with, as the squeezing done by it is too vigorous.

It is advisable to look at the specimens at the end of a day or two, and see how they are progressing. As likely as not, the blotting-paper will be soaked close to a juicy bloom, stalk or leaf, and, if it is not replaced by a dry piece, the specimen will be stained.

When the pressing, and, incidentally, when the drying is complete, the sprays should be mounted on cards or stiff sheets of paper. If fixed into a book, there must be a generous supply of guards or the volume will bulge.

Arrange one or more kindred specimens on a sheet, and fasten them down with little strips of gummed or pasted paper. Where the paper crosses over a stalk or leaf, it is not a bad plan to colour the part that hides the vegetation. In this way the strips do not show up too obviously.

Much of the value of a collection, of course, depends upon the classification adopted. To guard against putting members of one family along with others of very different families, it will be wise to follow the order and arrangements adopted by a good botany book.

Lastly, it may be well to add that a flower by itself is seldom as attractive as the flower with its stalk and typical foliage.

A CURIOUS SHOW OF FLOWERS

Here is a curious idea in plant growing. In the spring, cut a twig about 1 foot long from an elder or any other tree producing pithy stems. Split the stem from end to end and take out the pith. Put the two sections on a sheet of paper, lightly sprinkle seeds of annuals along the entire length of the two strips, cover with good loam that has been wetted to a paste, and then put the two strips together so that they fit as originally. Tie the two ends and here and there throughout the length with silk, and push the bigger end of the twig into a pot of loam. Water the loam and the twig occasionally. In time tiny plants will push their way out of the elder stem, and, in the summer, you will have a number of different flowers blossoming on the same branch.

THE COUNTRYSIDE ON THE TABLE

Youngsters love to spread out on the table their Noah's Ark inhabitants and make with them a miniature farm or other country settlement. Have you ever thought how simple it is to add to the realism of these toy arrangements ? Nothing, for instance, is easier than selecting in the garden small branched twigs to act as trees. With the bare twigs the trees appear to be in their winter garb, but if little pads of soft moss are pushed on to the tips of the twigs the trees look as they do in summer. Again, collect a number of twigs, all as stout as each other, tie them with black cotton, and so make two or three fences. Young children will be delighted with these little rustic models. For a third farmyard " property," take a sheet of cardboard, give it a coating of fish glue, and in the middle stick a small piece of ground glass, and elsewhere coat with granulated sugar. This stands for a frozen pond with snow all around. For a pond in summer, back an ordinary piece of glass with green paper, stick it to the card, and sift sand all around. It will adhere to the card if previously coated with fish glue, as before. These are merely a few suggestions—others will readily occur to any imaginative girl.

A Toy Tree Made of Twigs & Moss

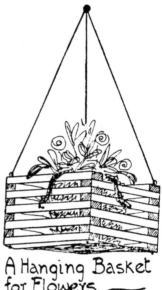

A Hanging Basket for Flowers. ——

A HANGING BASKET FOR FLOWERS

To make this attractive hanging flower basket, obtain 18 pieces of wood, each about a foot long, and 1 inch square in section. Fit them together, as shown in the sketch, by nailing the ends. Begin building up from the bottom. When the frame is assembled, nail a square of thin wood on the underface to serve as bottom. Lastly, fix a stout screw-eye at each upper corner and hang with four pieces of good stout wire. Fill with fibre in preference to garden mould.

A SMART SET OF BOOK-ENDS

You can easily make these attractive book-ends or supports. Take, first of all, a piece of cardboard, draw on it a square of 3 inches and, on all the sides, construct a rectangle, the dimensions of which are 3 by 6 inches.

Next, bend all the four rectangles upwards. Take one of them and stand it quite vertically. Then, make the opposite one lean on that which is already vertical and, from the latter, clip off the piece that stands up above the slanting rectangle. Bring the two opposite sides to a vertical position and cut off the portion of them that goes beyond the slanting rectangle. If all the pieces are now held in position, you have a shape like that shown in the diagram.

D

When you have satisfied yourself that the shape is correct, place the card flat on the table and paste a piece of grease-proof paper all over one of the faces. Now re-form the shape and bind it along the edges, but leave the vertical side, that is rectangular, undone for a little while. Obtain two pennyworth of putty and load it into the shape. Then, bind

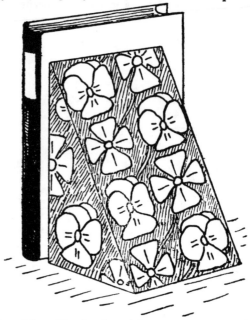

up the rectangular side. The book-end is now formed; but, before it can be considered complete, it must be decorated. A good plan is to cover it with the wallpaper of the room in which it is to serve or, better still, the cretonne which covers the chairs or hangs in the room, as curtains.

Naturally, you will require two of these ends, one for placing at each end of the row of books.

A SCRAP BOOK

Although a scrap book may not appeal very much to you, there are many children lying in hospital cots who would simply love to have one to while away some of their tedious moments. A month or two back, a nurse in one of the London hospitals suggested that we should make two or three such books for her tiny patients. Don't make them too bulky and heavy, she said, as the youngsters can't hold heavy ones. Make two thin ones rather than one heavy book, was her final injunction.

We started on the idea, but were, at first, a little puzzled to know where to obtain the necessary pictures. A look round the lumber room revealed a few old illustrated magazines. Yes, they certainly contained some pictures kiddies would like. We began to cut them out, then thought of some pretty advertisements we had put aside after visiting an exhibition. They too would do. Then the idea grew, and in no time we were snowed under with charming pictures and things which were lumber to us, but peeps in fairyland to poor little invalids in bed. There were magazine covers, old Christmas cards, pictorial advertisements, cigarette cards, picture post-cards, and hundreds of other illustrations.

We took some tough brown paper, cut it into sheets, the pages of which were a little larger than those of this book, put sixteen pages into each book, and bound them with ribbon. Then we pasted as many items as we could cram into each book. There was no cover. We were afterwards told that our efforts had afforded the tiny patients considerable delight.

Now here is a chance for you to do a useful act. Make some picture books like those described—you will surely not lack for suitable material —and send them to the matron of the nearest children's hospital, or to the children's ward of your local general hospital.

SMARTEN UP YOUR BOOK-SHELVES

If your books are looking untidy because some of the covers have been badly handled and others, in the first case, were flimsily bound, it will add to the attraction of your library if you give the books a jacket apiece of some smart wallpaper.

It may be that you can find some papers in the store cupboard, left over when various rooms were renovated but, if not, pay a visit to a wallpaper dealer and buy two or three rolls of different patterns. One roll, you will find, will give you the material for covering quite a number of books. Select patterns that are comparatively small and possessing plenty of colour.

To cover a book, place it on a sheet measuring an inch or two all round more than the book, and do not forget that you must allow for the thickness of the back. Fold the two vertical edges of the sheet around the covers and, then, run your fingers along the four horizontal edges. This will produce a slight crease which will guide you in the subsequent folding. Next, cut two wedge-shaped pieces, top and bottom, in the centre of the sheet, fold them inwards and thus shape the jacket to fit the back of the book. After that, tuck the four corners of the sheet under the horizontal edges of the book and bend over the flaps of paper.

The paper cover now fits the book, but to make it fit even better, take it off the book, place it flat on the table and run over all the folds with a ruler, the handle of a pocket-knife or anything smooth and handy. This will press the edges and make them lie nicely and snugly, when replaced on the book.

One thing remains to be done. Your jackets must bear the titles which they enclose, or it will be difficult to know which book is which. It is no use trying to print on the paper cover, because there is too much pattern. The best thing is to cut out a neat label, to inscribe it with the name of the book, also with the author's name if you like, and paste it high up on the back of the cover.

Your book-shelves will be an ornament to the room instead of being, perhaps, an eyesore.

BINDING MAGAZINE PARTS

Bookbinding is well within the powers of the average handy girl, if she is prepared to undertake a job that is exacting, and, at times, finicking.

We will say that you have a number of parts of the *Children's Book of*

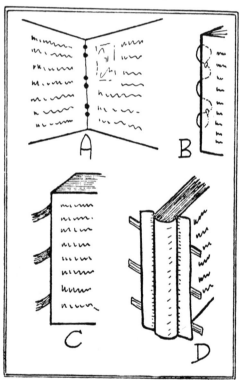

Knowledge, and you wish to bind them yourself. First, remove the paper covers and take out the pins that hold each part together. You will see that a part consists of a number of sections, and as there are eight parts to a volume, there are something like thirty-two sections in all. Take five or six sections, open them out to the middle pages, and arrange that all the top edges of the pages come level and the middle creases all super-imposed. Then force the point of an awl six times through the whole pile along the vertical crease (see A). This done, take one of the perforated sheets and place it over a few more sections, and force the awl through the pack, using the holes in the perforated sheet as a guide. In this way every section is perforated in exactly the same position.

Now take some strong white thread, and using the perforation holes sew each section as shown in B, but the loops are, of course, pulled tight. In the diagram they are left loose in order to show how they are made.

The next thing is to place all the sections in their correct order, one on top of the other, in a neat pile. Three lengths of strong tape are now passed through the loops, as shown in C. Next press the pile as close together as it will go, and glue a strip of canvas over the back (see D). Note that the back is first slightly curved.

The publisher's binding case is now obtained and placed round the mass of pages. The loose flaps of canvas and tape are glued to the inside covers, and a piece of clean paper is neatly pasted over them.

EMBROIDERY

A beginner in the art of embroidery should not attempt elaborate designs or stitches until she has first produced good work with the aid of transfer designs and the simpler stitches which are used for outlining.

Simplest of these is the *Running Stitch*. This may be used for outlining bold, simple designs ; it is advisable to use a fine silk or thread, of a colour contrasting with that of the ground material. Several rows of small regular running stitches look well as an embellishment to hems, cuffs, etc. ; work from the right to the left of the work. Wool may be used for working on heavy material, if desired, taking longer stitches than when working with silk.

Running Stitch

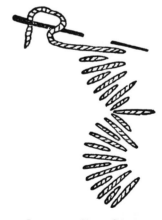

Long and Short Stitch

Long and Short Stitch —This stitch is most suitable for filling in solid pieces of embroidery, but it may also be used as an outlining stitch, if preferred. Work from the right to the left, the stitches being one long and one short alternately. Great care need not be taken to keep the work regular ; variety in the length of the stitches improves the effect.

Stem Stitch is useful for stalks, or for outlining when a running stitch is not suitable. It is worked in an upwards direction, that is, away from you. For each stitch the needle is placed a little beyond the previous stitch, passed through the material, and drawn out again half-way down the previous stitch and slightly to one side of it. Make the next stitch a little in advance of the previous one and curve it, if necessary, either to the right or left, in order to follow the slope of the outline. Do not make the stitches too long.

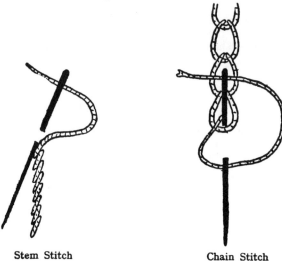

Stem Stitch   Chain Stitch

Chain Stitch. This is a very easy and quick method of outlining a design ; it may also be used to form the petals of a flower. Work towards you, or in a downward direction. Insert the needle in the material on the right side, pass it down and draw it through at a short distance below the spot where it was put in ; loop the thread round the point of the needle where it comes through the material on the right side, and hold the loop in place with the left thumb while you draw the needle through and thus tighten the thread of the loop. Keep to the lines of the design by inserting the point of the needle and drawing it out exactly on the line. Make each chain stitch overlap the previous one a little by inserting the needle, for each new stitch, at the point where it was drawn through to the right side when working the previous chain.

Satin Stitch. This is rather like stem stitch, but it is worked more closely and in straight rows, each stitch overlapping the previous one a little ; it is used for filling in solid spaces. As many rows as possible must be worked, side by side, until the space is covered. Work across the shorter width of a design whenever possible.

Cross Stitch. Spaces may be filled in very quickly by means of cross stitch. It may also be used for outlining on certain materials. If a transfer is used for the design to be worked, all that is necessary is to cover the outlines with cross stitch ; if, however, no transfer is being used, only coarsely woven material is suitable for this kind of embroidery, as it will be necessary to count the threads of the material in order to keep the stitches even and exactly the same size. Be careful to cross the stitches in the same direction throughout a design, otherwise the result will look untidy and irregular.

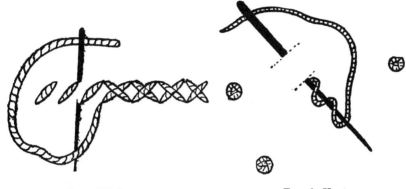

Cross Stitch   French Knot

French Knots. These may be used both for outlining or for filling in spaces. Bring the needle through to the right side of the material, wind the thread three times round the point of the needle and hold these twists in position by drawing tightly the portion of thread between the twists and the eye of the needle ; now place the point of the needle immediately beside the spot where it emerged from the material, and push it through to the wrong side, holding the thread firmly between the left finger and thumb until the needle and thread are drawn through to the wrong side—thus slipping the twist from the eye of the needle to form a knot on the right side of the material.

If these knots are required for an edging, they should be arranged at regular intervals along the lines of the design ; but if it is desired to fill in a space or a centre, they should be worked as closely together as possible in order to form a patch with no portions of the ground material showing between them.

Couching. Two kinds of thread are needed for this method of embroidering—one fine and one considerably thicker. When it is desired to work with wool, you will find that couching is an excellent method. The coarser thread must be laid quite flatly along the outline of the design—and wool is very suitable for this—while the thinner thread, either silk of a contrasting shade or a much finer wool, is used to secure the thicker thread in position. This is done by bringing the finer thread through from the wrong side to the right, passing it once over the strand of wool and drawing the needle through to the wrong side again at a spot immediately beside the spot where it was drawn up in the first place. Make another stitch in the same way, about half an inch further along the outline, and continue until the whole design has been ornamented. This method is suitable when the addition of a touch of colour to the neck and wrists of a dress is needed, or it may be used for outlining appliqué embroidery.

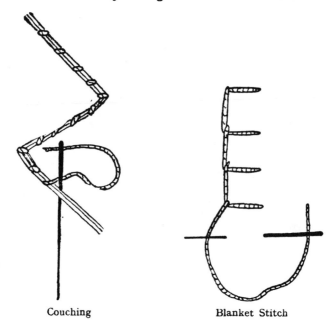

Couching   Blanket Stitch

Blanket Stitch. This may be used when a striking pattern is desired for outlining. Insert the needle from the underside of the material so that it may emerge on the right side at a point on the outline of the design. Start at the left hand and work towards the right. Put the needle a little to the right of where it emerged on the line to be embroidered, and a little above the line, pass it through and out again on the right side, immediately below where it was put in but exactly on the line, pass the thread round under the point of the needle, and hold it there with the left thumb, while you draw the needle and thread through. This makes the first stitch. The next must be about a quarter of an inch to the right of the first, and so on.

Buttonhole Stitch is another method which is frequently used for outlining purposes or for edging an appliqué design. This stitch is rather like blanket stitch, worked upside down and as closely as possible, there being no space between the stitches, while only a very small piece of material is picked up on the needle each time.

The various stitches described above may be used in many different ways for trimming purposes, in addition to outlining. For instance, large spots, if arranged regularly at intervals, may be used to introduce colour, when it is required, an elaborate embroidered design being not quite suitable. Draw the outline in pencil, of the required number of large spots or circles and then fill them in.

A large circle may be filled in with wool of various shades, arranging the stitches of each colour at a different angle from the stitches used for the adjacent colour. Wool or coarse silk may be used attractively in this way when a bold effect is desired. (See diagrams on page 33.)

For simple summer washing frocks there are many kinds of embroidery. The style used must depend on the material—whether it is patterned or

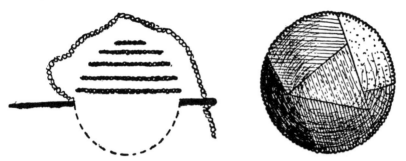

plain.   Any of the stitches described above may be used on plain material. It will be possible, however, for you yourself to design simple styles which will suit either checked ginghams, silks, etc., or plain linens.

By counting the lines or squares of the material a design may be arranged at regular intervals, either across a yoke or round a hem.   Use a linen thread, bright enough in colour to show up well against the background of the material.   Use the sides of the checks as guiding lines, and work each thread over one square and under the next ; then go in the reverse direction—that is, work under the portion of material over

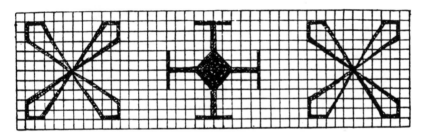

which you previously worked, and over the spaces which have been left blank.   In this way a continuous outline of thread is produced.   When triangles appear in your design, they may be filled in solidly in order to emphasise the pattern.

Some materials of a fluffy nature may be embroidered in wools, using the same kind of design as for ginghams and linens.   Transfer or draw a design on the material, then place a long strand of wool along the outlines and stitch it down by means of a silk thread of a contrasting shade.   The wool does not need to be threaded into a needle at all, the only stitching necessary is done by the silk ; be careful to secure the wool firmly by means of silk stitches whenever it is necessary to turn a corner or sharp curve.

A daisy is a conventional little flower which can be drawn by hand very easily and embroidered in a number of different ways.

In a coarse linen thread, or wool, it may be worked on cushion covers, table runners, etc., or in fine silk or washing thread it may be added as a decoration for jumpers, children's dresses, etc.

E

Decide on the size design you want ; then, by means of a pair of compasses and a pencil, lightly draw a number of circles, of the same size, on the material to be embroidered. In the centre of each circle. draw another one, much smaller, to act as the centre of the flower. The petals of the daisy must be outlined faintly, within the larger circle. Arrange them so that the outside points of the petals come on the circumference of the larger circle, while the other ends of the petals touch the smaller pencilled circle. Draw as many petals as possible without overcrowding ; stalks and leaves may be added if you like, but the flowers, alone, can be made to look sufficiently ornamental without any additions.

The petals are most easily and quickly worked by making one long chain stitch to each petal, with a smaller chain stitch of another shade just inside the larger one. The small circle in the centre should be made of bright yellow French knots or filled in with satin stitch of the same shade. If you are adding stalks, these should be of stem stitch, while the leaves may be filled in either with satin stitch or long and short stitch. (See diagram below.)

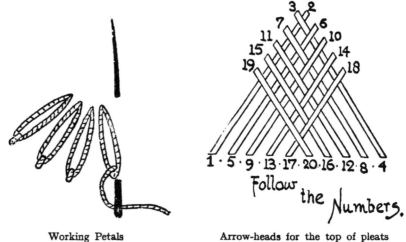

Working Petals   Arrow-heads for the top of pleats

Arrow-heads for the top of pleats. First outline a triangle on the material with a tacking thread, then thread a needle with some silk to match the material. Bring the needle through the wrong side, at the left-hand corner of the triangle, draw the silk through and push the needle through to the wrong side at the top point of the triangle. Do the same from the right hand corner of the triangle.

The next stitch starts immediately to the right of the left corner and finishes just below the point of the triangle, on the right side of it. Do the same from a spot immediately to the left of the right corner, and finish it just below the point of the triangle, on the left side of it. Make several more stitches like this, doing first one on the left and the next on the right, until only a small triangle is left uncovered in the centre of the base of the large triangle. Fill in this space with the same coloured silk, making the first stitch along the base of the triangle ; start this stitch beside those which filled the left side of the arrowhead and finish it beside the right-hand stitches. Place the next immediately above it, only it will be a little shorter than the previous one. Continue making each one shorter than the one before until the last is merely a dot of silk.

APPLIQUÉ EMBROIDERY

If you have a plain washing dress of which you have tired, try your hand at appliqué embroidery ; perhaps, then, you will think twice before consigning the dress to the old clothes basket.

To do appliqué is not at all difficult, and if you are content with simple patterns, no transfer designs will be needed. First, take a look round and see if you can find some suitable pieces of material—quite small ones will do very well. Coloured linen or brown holland will look best on cotton washing frocks, while ribbon or bits of silk may be used for silk and woollen frocks. Use a rather coarse linen thread, or wool, for stitching on the design—select that which best suits the material of the dress.

Draw a simple pattern first on paper, and cut it out round the edges ; place this cut-out pattern on the dress to see if it is suitable, and decide where it may best be placed. If it is not the right size, cut out other patterns until you have one which seems just right. A plain square placed at intervals round the hem of a frock or at the neck will entirely alter its appearance if made of bright, attractive colours.

When you have decided on the design, place the pattern on the pieces of material which you have selected to form the appliqué. Cut out as many shapes as you think will be required, and tack each piece carefully in position on the garment. When all the designs have been arranged satisfactorily, turn the edges under as narrowly as possible, and oversew* each one securely to the dress, with a fine cotton to match the material of the dress.

There are many stitches suitable for outlining these appliqué designs. A simple, quick and effective one is blanket stitch described on page 32. It shows up well if worked in wool, either of a bright shade which will tone with the dress, or of the same shade ; take care, however, that the colour of the stitches is not the same as that of the designs appliquéd ; if they are too nearly alike, the effect of the outlining will be weakened.

Start by inserting the needle on the wrong side of the work ; draw it through to the right side so that the needle emerges on the outside edge of the oversewing stitches. Then pass the needle through the design a little above this edge, but to the right, and draw it out again immediately below the point where it was pushed in, but exactly on the line of over-sewing. Loop the thread from the first stitch under the point of the needle, and hold it there with the left thumb while you draw the point of the needle through the loop, thus causing the thread to be drawn up tightly.

Make the next stitch in the same way, passing the needle through the design a little to the right of the previous stitch and a little above the line of over-sewing ; thrust it through directly below the point where it went in, but on the line of oversewing. Loop the thread round the

* See Plain Sewing, page 100.

point of the needle and draw the needle and thread through.   Continue in the same way all round the edge of the appliqué design.

Small children's clothes may be made to look charming if little animals or flowers, of rather startling colours, are appliquéd at various points on overalls or frocks.   If you are clever enough to draw these yourself, do so.   The outline must be drawn on the material of which the appliqué is to be made ; it must then be cut out and dealt with in the way already described.   If, on the other hand, you are unable to draw well, you may overcome the difficulty by buying transfers of the patterns you prefer. A hot iron must be used to transfer this design from the paper to the brightly coloured material which is to be used for the appliqué ; when this has been done, cut it out round the edge and then proceed as before,

but for this type of design blanket stitch should not be used.

Couching is one of the easiest methods of outlining and this would be excellent for edging an animal or flower design.   Use two or three threads of silk, or wool ; knot the end securely, and from the wrong side bring it through to the right somewhere along the outline of the design.   Draw it, now, over the outline, and fasten it in position by oversewing it at intervals of about a half or a quarter of an inch, with either a finer wool of a different colour, or with fine silk.

There are many other ways of edging appliqué embroidery.   Buttonhole stitch, running stitch, cross stitch and others have been described on pages 29 to 32.   Any of these may be used instead of blanket stitch or couching, if preferred.

It would be useless to attempt to enumerate all the classes of articles for which appliqué embroidery is suitable, but plain lamp shades, linen bibs, handbags, nightdress or pyjama cases, etc., are all subjects which may be decorated in this way.   Some of these are sure to be found in your home.

A wet afternoon, which might otherwise prove rather boring, may be well spent in making preliminary attempts at this kind of embroidery, on whatever articles of this kind that you may find near at hand.

When you have had a few small successes, more elaborate decoration, and on a larger scale, may be undertaken.   The cushions in the conservatory or sun-parlour might do with a little improvement.   Do not go to the trouble of making a whole set of new covers for them.   Bright strips of casement cloth, or bands of coloured ribbon will entirely change the scheme of decoration, if appliquéd to cushions, table-covers, etc., by means of any of the outlining stitches already described.

AN AFTERNOON TEA CLOTH IN CROSS-STITCH

A smart afternoon tea-cloth may be made by embroidering in coloured cross stitch on coarsely woven coloured linen. If a white ground is preferred, a coarse canvas may be used, on which cross stitch can be worked without using a transfer. If, however, you have chosen a material which is so fine that the threads can only be counted with difficulty, then a transfer design must be ironed on to the material, and the cross stitch pattern worked over this.

Assuming that you are using a coarse material, and will need no

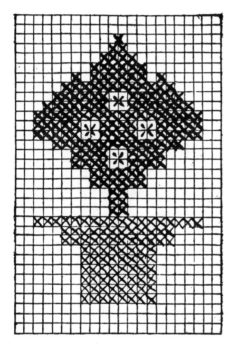

transfer, it will first be necessary to decide on a design, either of your own invention, or a copy of one already worked on something else. Make up your mind what style of pattern you prefer, either geometrical, conventional or floral, and using graph-paper as a background, pencil in the outlines of a cross stitch design. When you have produced a pleasing scheme, it will not be difficult to work it on the linen or on the canvas direct, being careful to count the threads in order to keep the stitches a regular size ; always cross the threads in the same direction.

When the embroidery has been worked, finish off the edges of the cloth by hem-stitching (page 98) all round, in coloured thread to match the scheme of the embroidery. A mercerised cotton is suitable for this, or a fine linen thread. These may be obtained in a wide variety of colours, and they wash well.

If this cloth proves a success, you might make a tray-cloth of the same material, to match. These would make a lovely Christmas or wedding present, and would cost very little to make.

AN EMBROIDERED TOWEL

Hemstitched huckaback towels are an essential item in the store of house-linen. Embroidered towels are considered a luxury, yet the most ornamental towel made at home costs less than the ordinary plain hemstitched article bought at a shop. Make one for your mother and see if she is not pleased.

You need 1¼ yards of plain huckaback towelling and a strip of crochet insertion 2 inches longer than the width of the towel. The pattern of crochet described above has been suggested, as it is simple and quickly made.

First, see that each end of the linen has been cut perfectly straight, and if it has not, trim off the uneven parts. 2 inches from one end draw 6 or 7 threads right across the width of the towel. Turn up the edge narrowly, and then fold over as far as the drawn threads, making a 1 inch hem. Tack it along to keep it level, and hemstitch neatly along the drawn threads.

Sew one side of the crochet insertion firmly to the extreme edge of this hem. Be very careful not to drag the crochet, as when washed it will shrink considerably. It is advisable to use 2 inches more insertion than the width of the towel; this will enable you to sew it on a little full.

From the other end of the towel cut a perfectly straight piece of linen, about 3 inches wide. Turn each cut edge in about ¼ inch on the same side of the material, place the two edges together and tack along. To this double edge of linen sew the other edge of the strip of insertion, thus completing one end of the towel.

Three inches from the other end of the linen draw 6 or 7 threads; turn in the raw edge and tack it along the drawn threads, making a 1½ inch hem. Finish with hemstitching along the drawn threads.

A BUTTON-HOLE OF SILK OR WOOLLEN FLOWERS

These dainty little bunches of flowers are made with fine wire and wool, which must not be too thick. If preferred, embroidery silk may be used instead of wool. For each petal, a wire shape must first be made; four or five will be needed for each flower.

Take a piece of wire, 4 or 5 inches long, and bend one end round in a loop, making it quite firm by twisting the shorter end securely round the longer end—the loop is intended for a petal. Thread a darning needle with a long strand of wool of the shade selected for the flower, wind it several times round the long end of wire which is intended for the stalk, then take it up from the bottom of the petal to the top, passing it over the centre of the wire loop, and fixing it in position by stitching once or twice on each side.

The petal now requires to be darned ; this is done by passing the needle first under the centre wool strand, then over, round and under the wire at one side ; bring it up again and over the centre wool thread, then under, round and over the other wire side ; continue in this way until the petal is darned from top to bottom, then wind the wool round the wire stalk several times and knot it before breaking off.

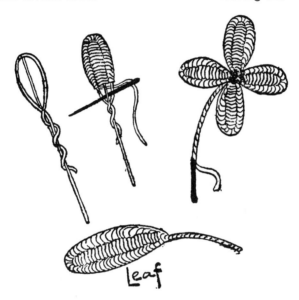

Make as many petals of the same colour as are required for a flower. Gather them together, winding the wire stalks round each other ; then take a length of green wool, stitch it firmly to the back of the flower, and wind it closely round the twist of wires, to form the stem. Finish it securely at the end. Bend back the petals to resemble an open flower, and fill in the centre with a tight mass of yellow French knots of either silk or wool. Make more flowers of different shades.

Leaves may be worked in the same way, but make the wire loop twice as large as those used for the petals, and bend it so that it is long and narrow. Use green wool or silk, for the centre thread and darn it with green. Two or three leaves arranged behind a bunch of various coloured flowers will form a smart little buttonhole.

AN ALMS BAG

If you are a church worker and are good with your needle, you would probably like to make one or more alms bags for the collections. We give a design which you may care to imitate. The height from top to bottom should be about 7 inches, and the width about 5 inches. The material may be a heavy velvet or sateen of a dark colour, such as deep

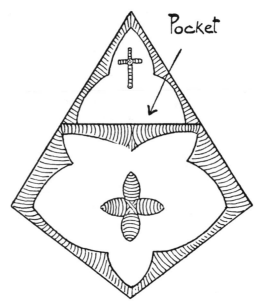

Pocket

violet, maroon, black or blue.   Naturally, the inside of the bag will be lined and so will be the back.   Use sateen for the purpose.
The design and the edging are worked in silks.

PRETTY LITTLE LABELS AND THINGS

If you are one of those girls who like to do things neatly, here are a few ideas which may help you in your praiseworthy endeavours.

When doing up Christmas parcels, make some pretty labels bearing seasonable motifs, and tie them on for the addresses.   If the packages have to go through the post, use ordinary tie-on labels, but draw and colour a border of holly and mistletoe around them.   If the parcels are delivered by hand, let the tie-on label be more artistic.   We suggest a large holly leaf, cut out to shape, with a trio of berries placed where the string is run through.   Colour the whole of the leaf green, and the berries a bright red.

The string for doing up the parcels may be enlivened by being dipped in red and green ink, and then left to dry.

When parcels are intended for children, the tie-on labels may be cut-out pictures of Father Christmas, and other festive characters.   One side should be devoted to a coloured representation of the selected individual, while the other is reserved for the address.

Ornamental notepaper is usually not in good taste, but an exception is made in the case of paper used for sending out or accepting party invitations.   In the top left-hand corner of the sheet draw something indicative of party-fun.   A nicely coloured cracker, a pair of evening shoes, a table loaded with cakes and sweets, or even a plum pudding with a sprig of holly, will be just the thing.

When you invite a large number of friends to dinner or supper, there is always a certain amount of confusion in the guests finding the seats allotted to them. Why not make little ornamental cards and write a name on each ? This will save much of the fuss which is sure to happen if the seats are not named. The illustration we give is merely one suggestion for a suitable design. You will be able to think of dozens yourself. If the pattern you choose entails a cut-out shape, cut four or five together before you do any of the pen or brush ornamentation. It will save a good deal of labour.

Menu cards will offer a good deal of scope for your artistic abilities. As a number will be required, all alike, it may be advisable to run off sufficient copies from a duplicating machine, and then paint the design. Let the design form part of the duplicated matter, for the colouring will then be much easier. Use glazed paper so that the colours will not run, but, in order to avoid smudging the duplicating ink, place each copy on blotting paper as it comes from the machine.

Another way of providing a batch of menus is to run off sufficient duplicated copies on the usual duplicating paper, and then to affix a fair sized seal to the top left-hand corner. Cut the seal out of bright coloured paper, and print some suitable greeting on it.

In the above notes, we have merely suggested general ideas. A girl who is attracted by these hints can develop them considerably. For instance, she may care to make her Christmas parcels look far more attractive than described at the outset of this chapter. She may decide to use bright paper for the wrapping, to tie them with dainty ribbon, to band the faces of the boxes with lengths of narrow paper frieze, drawn and coloured by herself, and to fix seals, here and there, on them of her own making.

A SURPRISE GIFT CONTAINER

On Christmas Day and at parties, it is often the custom to shower a number of small gifts on the younger members who are present. A very pleasing way of disposing of the gifts is to put them in a container which is hung up in some accessible position. A number of strings are attached to the lower part of the container and these are held by chosen members of the little band. On giving the signal, the strings are pulled, the bottom falls out of the receptacle, and the presents are showered on the expectant company.

Naturally, the container must be strongly attached to the ceiling and, also, it will be unwise to place any gifts in the container which might break, on falling.

The receptacle is made by bending a piece of cardboard into a cylinder, pinning it along the overlapping edges with three or four paper fasteners and covering the cardboard with crêpe paper of a gay colour. The paper continues several inches below the lower edge of the cylinder and it is bunched together, as shown in the diagram. A ring of holes is stabbed through the paper, so that it will tear easily on being tugged.

The gifts are put into the container by way of the top opening.

SILVER AND GOLD

Unless you are already acquainted with this charming form of decoration, you will be surprised at the wonderful effects which can be obtained in a very easy manner.

First of all, you must gather together a collection of pieces of silver paper with gold and coloured designs on them. Some of them, which you will find wrapped round chocolates, are extremely attractive and the more beautiful the ones you come across, the finer will be the work which is in store for you.

When you have a number of pieces, flatten out all the creases and, then, cut them into sections no bigger than a postage-stamp, but make them various odd shapes.

Next, go to one of the sixpenny stores and purchase a small glass bowl. Select one that bears no pattern of any kind, neither engraved nor cut, and, if possible, without feet. Then, with a bottle of gum, dab a small quantity of adhesive on the front side of the pieces of silver paper and stick them on the outside of the bowl. Place the pieces so that they overlap slightly, and be careful that, when you have finished, no part of the glass is uncovered.

Leave the bowl for a few days and, then, coat the back of the silvered papers with a cellulose enamel or some stove black. The latter is, probably, preferable. You now have a delightful bowl, the glass of which makes the multi-coloured papers sparkle in a most attractive manner.

Of course, you may cover the inside instead of the outside of the bowl and, with a little planning, produce a variety of charming effects.

A PRESENT FOR FATHER

Would you like to make your father or grown-up brother a useful and attractive birthday or Christmas present ? If so, why not try your hand with an ornamental pad of shaving papers ? The work is quite easy, the materials are by no means expensive, and the article is of daily use.

The first thing to do, if you decide to make one, is to procure a supply of thin paper. We recommend ordinary typewriting paper cut into four. If the paper can be obtained in assorted colours so much the better. Having cut about twenty-five sheets, each into four, and arranged them into a neat little stack, the next thing is to get a piece of stout card slightly larger all round than the size of each sheet of paper. Cover this, both back and front, with a strip of gay coloured cretonne, turn in the raw edges, and sew down with a neat stitch. Now take a sheet of drawing paper, the size of the shaving sheets, and paint some suitable picture or design—your father's initials, for instance, or if it is to be a Christmas present, a scene depicting the Wise Men of the East on camels. Place this drawing on the top of the pack of shaving papers, put the pack centrally on the cretonne-covered card, and through the top corner drive an awl. Through the pierced hole thread a piece of coloured string, and, if you like, a piece of ribbon as well. Tie the string tightly, and shape the ribbon into a neat bow. You now have an acceptable present, which most men will find very useful.

RAINBOW MATERIAL

Rainbow material has countless uses. You may be in need of a multi-coloured scarf, a short curtain of jazz colours for a small book-shelf, a startling covering for a sunshade, etc. This effect may be obtained easily by using plain materials and three or four packets of dye.

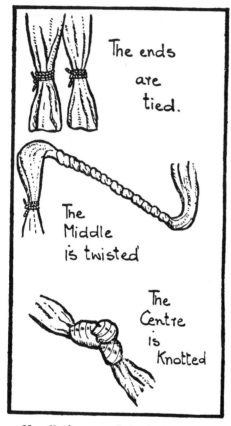

The ends are tied.

The Middle is twisted

The Centre is Knotted

Let us say that you have a length of white crêpe-de-chine and you want to make a rainbow scarf. Any thin material will, of course, do equally well, but there is one exception and that is artificial silk, which is best left alone.

First, procure three packets of dye. They should be distinct colours such as orange, green and purple. Dissolve them separately in three jam jars, using boiling water.

Now, take the scarf and bunch up each end separately and tie a piece of thin string tightly around each. Dip the ends into the orange dye. Immerse them to about an inch above the string. Remove and rinse in cold water.

Next, take the scarf and twist it tightly in a plaited fashion between the two tied ends. Dip this part in the same dye. Remove and rinse in cold water.

We now unroll the scarf and retwist it tightly; then dip it in the green dye. Remove and rinse in cold water.

Unroll the material, tie in two places, and dip each of these knots in the purple dye. Remove and rinse in cold water.

Now, cut the strings, pull the material open, dip in cold water, squeeze out, dry and iron. You have a delightful piece of jazz crêpe-de-chine.

Take the scarf and note how the colouring has affected certain parts : for instance, the ends will be mostly orange coloured because we dipped the tied ends in the orange dye. If you prefer green or purple ends, reverse the order in which the shades are used.

WHERE ARE THE SCISSORS

Yes, where are they ? The wise old owl does not want to be told ; they are in front of his nose all the time.

If you live in a house where scissors are everlastingly disappearing, make this unique head of an owl. Cut out a piece of cardboard to conform with the shape, and cover the upper part with any white material, but preferably velvet, and the lower part with some corresponding black material. Before fitting the stuff to the card, make the

eyes and edging with black silk, and fit a little calico bag, on the reverse side of the body-piece, to take the point of the scissors. Cut a small slit (see illustration) to admit the scissors to the bag, from the front.

Hang up this head in a suitable place.

POPPY-HEAD ORNAMENTS

In the winter, when flowers for indoor decoration are scarce, it is a good plan to turn to poppy heads and use them for ornamental purposes. If there are any large heads forming in the garden during the autumn, pick them as soon as they are ripe, and hang them in bunches, upside down, in a dark corner until required. If no such supplies are available, buy heads at the chemist's for a few pence each, perforate the base of the heads, and fit dried stems of shrubs and so provide stalks. The poppy heads, when dry, range from an uninviting blue-green to dull brown. To make them attractive, mix some oil paints of vivid colours with plenty of turpentine and coat each head. Paint the surfaces in bands, rings, lozenges, etc., and coat the stems, preferably with green, brown, or white. With a little scheming some really delightful effects may be produced, and the heads will prove attractive all the winter.

DECORATING EGGS FOR EASTER

Why not decorate the eggs which are brought to the breakfast table on Easter Sunday ? It is a custom that has died out in this country, but it is still practised abroad, in France and Belgium.

Suppose you would like some boiled eggs to have green shells. Take a handful of parsley and put it in water, leaving it there for a full day.

When the eggs are to be boiled, use the parsley water, and they will come up to table a beautiful green. A light red hue is provided by boiling the eggs in vinegar, containing the flesh of a mashed beetroot. Yellow shells may be obtained by putting onion skins into the water used for boiling the eggs. No unpleasant flavour will be imparted to the eggs themselves.

Another and perhaps more artistic effect is obtained by painting designs, initials, etc., on the shells with a brush, dipped in a little melted lard. Allow the lard to harden and then immerse the eggs for half an hour in vinegar. At the end of this time, the acid will have eaten slightly into the shells, everywhere but where the lard acted as a protection. Your design will therefore stand up in relief. Write the names of your small brothers and sisters in this way on their breakfast eggs, and note their expressions of surprise.

HOW TO MAKE DECORATIONS FROM EGG SHELLS

There are numerous odd uses for egg shells, yet we are continually throwing so many of them away. They may be made into presents or saleable bazaar oddities by drawing features upon them, dressing them in little hats, and mounting them on pen-wipers or paper-weights.

Egg shell medallions and castings may be made by thoroughly baking the shells, beating them to a fine powder, and mixing with gum arabic solution and white of egg. This can be made to about the consistency of dough, and cast or moulded into any shape or form you fancy and then finally dried in the sun.

Eggs for decoration should either be blown or have a portion sawn off with a fine saw. If it is necessary to make them reasonably durable, they may be filled with melted resin or wax, or even a wood-paste. If blown with holes at both ends, cords may be run through before the interior is filled, and the egg decorated ; with a tassel at one end it could be used as a bell-pull. This is illustrated, and it is an example of what can be done with an egg shell.

A TELEPHONE COVER

A telephone is about as ugly as it is useful, and any scheme which is successful in hiding it or making it look like something else is worth considering.

The accompanying illustration shows a very acceptable way of covering over the inartistic though useful fittings. The foundation of this doll-like being is the wire frame of a lamp shade. The head and upper part of the body can be bought at fancy drapers, where fittings for tea cosies are sold. The hat is a shaped piece of buckram and the skirt is made of four strips of cretonne. The feet are merely two dangling pieces of white material, suitably shaped and outlined ; they are sewn to the

sides of the frame. They do not serve any very useful purpose and may reasonably be omitted, if preferred.

The inside must be lined with as few folds as possible, otherwise the material will catch on the telephone when the doll is lifted off.

" NUMBER, PLEASE ? "

Looking for a needle in a bundle of hay is an easy job compared with hunting for a telephone number in the directory, especially if you are in a hurry. Of course, the correct thing is to have a personal index of all the people whom you ring up frequently. Such a list should be arranged alphabetically, it should be easy to consult and it ought to hang up beside the 'phone, where it can be sought in a moment.

Here is a very useful telephone list which answers all these requirements. Cut a piece of stout card, ten by four inches. Place it on the work-table. with the shorter side horizontal, and paste a piece of drawing

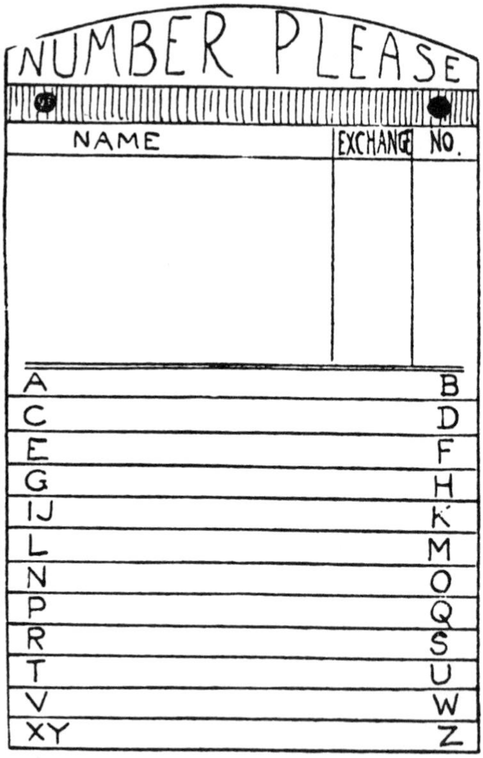

paper, two inches wide, along the upper edge. On this strip, draw and colour some ornamental design or simply print on it the title to this paragraph, " Number, Please ? " Then take twelve sheets of paper, all four inches wide, but the first has to be four inches long ; the second, 4¼, the third 4½, and so on. Glue the upper edge of each to a strip of wide tape, so that about an inch of the tape projects, all along, above the sheet of paper. Thus, each piece of paper is given a flexible hinge.

Now, take the twelve sheets and rule each of them with three columns, as shown in the diagram, giving them the titles : (a) Name, (b) Exchange, (c) Number. Do this on the back and front but let one face be upside-down in relation to the other. You will see the reason for this, presently. On the side of each sheet which you decide is to be the front, reserve a space of a quarter of an inch along the bottom for taking the initial letters.

The next step is to pile up all the twelve sheets, the shortest at the top, the others, graduated throughout, and arrange that the tapes are one above the other. Then, cut a piece of good brown paper to cover over all the top sheet, except the bottom edge, bearing the initial letters. Having done this, fix all the sheets to the cardboard by running two paper fasteners through the pile of tapes and the card itself. Turn down the wings of the fasteners at the back of the card. The telephone list is now finished.

From the diagram, it will be seen that all the initial letters are clearly in view. Letters recorded on the left are entered on the front of the sheet ; those on the right, at the back of the sheet, i.e., the sheet must be lifted up. That is why the ruling on the backs of the sheets was inverted. Note that I and J, and X and Y are placed together because I and X are seldom found as initial letters of surnames. The tape hinge given to each sheet, enables the sheet to be raised without any trouble and it falls limply and does not bulge out, when released.

THE HOME MAGAZINE

One of our most cherished possessions is a little, very amateurishly bound volume, about an inch think. We would not part with it for worlds, because it is something we did, week by week, when we were very small. It was like this. One day, the idea came to us to " publish " a magazine of our very own. We first of all selected a title. It was the one printed at the head of this paragraph. For the paper, we folded a sheet from an exercise book into four and two such sheets, making sixteen pages, constituted a number. The magazine came out every week, and we never missed for two years while the publication lasted. Each issue was numbered and dated and the pages were numbered consecutively throughout a volume, which consisted of thirteen copies. Then another volume began. We must have been very thorough, because the last line of every issue bore the statement " Printed and Published by so and so at so and so, etc.," in order to conform with the law.

The matter used for filling up the pages consisted mainly of a record of the events which happened in our house. The members of the family were given assumed names, which were adhered to throughout. Any little expedition that we made was written-up into an article, and places we happened to visit were described. The magazine was fully illustrated, to use a publisher's term, the one on the front page always being in colour. There was an instalment of a continued tale in each number which was the only piece of fiction permitted. Perhaps that was as well, because our *present* view is that it was the poorest stuff we ever attempted.

When a volume came to a close, all the numbers forming it were stitched, and then glued by means of tapes and end papers to a cardboard cover. On the back, a little label was pasted, bearing the inscription " The Home Magazine," Vol. I," or whatever the number was.

Our reason for putting all these facts on record is merely to pass on

G

the idea to other girls. It strikes us as a capital piece of work for any youthful person to undertake. We derived great fun from it, it kept us from being idle, and it helped us to learn how to put our thoughts sensibly into words. Why not start a magazine of your own ?

Perhaps we ought to say in conclusion that one copy only of each issue was published, and it was all printed by hand.

A USEFUL PIN-CUSHION

Cut out two circles of leather, 2 inches in diameter, and of a fairly stout substance. Then, obtain some felt, as thick as possible. The grade sold by furnishers for floor coverings is what you want. Cut two rounds of this material, also 2 inches in diameter. Put the two pieces of felt together, one exactly over the other, and sew them together along the edges which touch.

Having done all this, put one piece of leather on top of the felt, and

the other piece below it, taking care that the face side of the leather is outwards in both cases. Then, drive a hole through the centre of the entire pack. This can be done by means of an awl, a large needle or even by forcing the leg of a compass through.

While the awl, or whatever you use, is still gripping the four thicknesses, get a piece of silk cord, make a loop in it, and then pull out the awl and thread the two ends of the cord through the hole. When they emerge on the under-side, tie them into a knot and, then, make a neat bow or fit two small tassels.

This makes a very useful pin-cushion. The pins are pushed into the edges of the felt and the silk loop enables you to hang up the cushion, so that it can always be found when wanted.

POSIES MADE OF BEECH-MASTS

One day in the autumn, when you are out in the country, hunt around for some beech-masts. They are usually to be found in quantities in woods that are composed of beech trees.

When you reach home, break off the stalks to within about half an inch of the woody cup, if the stalks are brittle, and make imitation stalks of thin flower wire, but use several thicknesses, which will have to be plaited. If the stalks are not brittle—they generally are, however —there is no need to supply artificial ones.

Next, take the masts and dip them in some coloured ink or dye. Choose a rich reddy-brown tint for some and a blackish brown for others. Then hang them up to drain and dry, for a day or two.

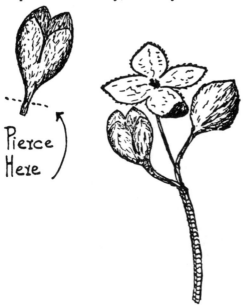

Pierce Here

At the end of this time, bind the wire stalks with strips of thin clinging material, to match the colour of the beech-masts, and make up the posies, each comprising seven or eight masts. Make the posies of masts all one colour or of assorted colours, as you please. If you care to brush some gold paint over a few specimens, they will look very smart, when bound up with the brown masts; but a whole posy of gilt masts seldom looks neat.

A POSY OF BUTTONS

Have you ever thought of making yourself an attractive button-hole of buttons? It sounds rather funny, doesn't it, almost a tongue twister? But the question is "Have you?"

Go through the family store of odd buttons and pick out about a dozen bone ones—those with holes in them and no shanks. Then, thread a six inch length of flower wire through each, bring the ends together and give them a twist so that they cannot fall off.

Now, dip each button in some well-stirred cellulose paint, and hang them all on a line of string to dry, with a sheet of newspaper underneath. If you have chosen three or four bright colours and assemble about nine or ten buttons together of varied hues, they will make a charming posy for your buttonhole.

On drying, the buttons should be neatly arranged together, all the wires should be plaited into one stalk, when a strip of black tape will bind them neatly.

POSIES MADE OF CLOTH

Can you find some coloured pieces of cloth ? Even small snippets will do, if you can get a few large pieces as well. Cut them up into circles with ordinary edges, with wavy edges, with pointed edges, etc. Let most of the circles be about three-quarters of an inch in diameter, but have a few larger and smaller ones, also.

Now, begin to assemble the shapes. As a rule, put them in twos, a large one behind a small one, and stitch them together in the middle.

When you have done a number in this way, assemble them, without any idea of geometrical or symmetrical design, and stitch them to a round of cloth, with a scalloped edge and about 3 inches in diameter. In this simple manner, you can make some delightful posies for your buttonhole.

The finest effects are obtained by keeping similar colours as far apart from each other as possible.

KNITTING

The same remarks may be made as to the selection of wools and needles, as are made in the Section on Crochet, page 85. The size of a piece of work, and the number of stitches required to be cast on, will depend largely on the tension at which you work, and you must vary the size of the needles you use according to your own manner of knitting, which may be either tightly or loosely.

TO CAST ON

Leave free an end of wool long enough to work the number of stitches required, then make a loop on one needle. Hold the needle with the right hand. Take the free end of wool in the left hand, and twist it round the left thumb, making a loop ; pass the point of the needle under this loop, and with the right hand, pass the wool (from the ball) round the point of the needle, and draw this through the loop on the left thumb, thus making a second loop on the right-hand needle. Draw up the free wool, not too tightly, thus tightening the loop on the needle.

Cast on the next stitch by winding the free end of wool again round the left thumb and continue as before. Repeat until the required number of stitches has been cast on.

PLAIN KNITTING OR GARTER STITCH

Cast on the reqaired number of stitches. Hold the needle containing the stitches with the left hand, and with the right hand put the other needle, from the front, through the first stitch on the left-hand needle. Pass the free end of the wool round the point of the needle in the right hand, as in diagram, keeping the wool at the back of the work, and with the point of the needle draw the wool back through the stitch to the front.

Keep this stitch on the right-hand needle, and from the left-hand needle slip the stitch through which you have worked.

Continue with each stitch in this manner, until all have been passed from the left-hand needle to the right-hand needle. The next row is worked in just the same way, but first change the needles, so that the right-hand one, holding the stitches, is now held in the left hand, while the left-hand one is used by the right hand to knit the row.

PURL KNITTING

Cast on the required number of stitches and hold the needle containing them in the left hand as for plain knitting. Keep the wool at the front

of the work. Put the point of the right-hand needle through the first stitch on the left-hand needle, but pass it from the back of the loop to the front, not from front to back as in plain knitting. Pass the wool round the point of the right-hand needle, and bring it under and to the front again; draw the wool through the stitch on the left-hand needle to the back of the work, and keep the stitch so made on the right-hand needle, while you slip the stitch through which you have worked from the left-hand needle. Continue in this way with each stitch until all are passed from the left to the right-hand needle.

TO MAKE A STITCH IN KNITTING

It is sometimes necessary to increase the number of stitches on a needle—this is done by making an extra stitch at intervals. To do this, bring the wool forward between the needles and wind it once round the right-hand needle, making a loop. Knit the next stitch as usual, and continue to the end of the row. When this loop is reached in the next row, it must be treated as a stitch and knitted into, thus adding one to the number of stitches on the needles.

TO SLIP A STITCH IN KNITTING

Put the right-hand needle into the stitch which is to be knitted next, but instead of knitting it, slip it from the left-hand needle to the right-hand.

STOCKING STITCH IN KNITTING

This is the form of knitting most frequently used for coats, sweaters, etc. All the stitches on the right side of the work are plain knitting, and all those on the back are purl.

If you are making a circular piece of work on four needles, such as socks, stockings and some kinds of jumpers, you have only to work plain

knitting all the time. But if you are working with two needles, and it is necessary to turn the work at the end of each row, then the rows must be worked alternately plain and purl. This gives the all-plain-knitting effect on the right side of the work, and all-purl on the wrong side. If you look at the inside of a plain stocking, you will see that every row is purl stitch.

MOSS STITCH IN KNITTING

This consists of plain and purl stitches alternately. Knit the first row with 1 plain, 1 purl, to the end of the row; turn and start the next row with the same stitch as the last one of the previous row; that is, if the last stitch was a purl, on the right side, then the first stitch of the next row must be worked as a purl on the wrong side, the next one plain, and so on to the end of the row. Work each row in the same way. This produces the alternate 1 plain, 1 purl pattern in the up and down way of the knitting, as well as in the horizontal way.

GRAFTING IN KNITTING

Grafting is used when it is necessary to join two pieces of knitting, and it is desirable that there should be no seam where the join is made.

The stitches must be divided equally on two needles; place the needles together so that the end of the wool is at the right end of the back needle, and hold them both with the left hand. Thread the end of the wool through a bodkin or a blunt large-eyed needle. Pass the needle through the first loop on the front needle, as if to knit one purl, but do not slip the stitch from the knitting needle; draw the wool through this stitch, then pass the bodkin through the first stitch on the back needle, as if to knit plain, but do not slip the stitch from the knitting needle— draw the wool right through.

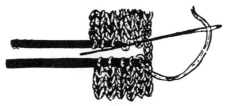

Now pass the bodkin through the first stitch on the front needle, as in plain knitting, and slip it from the knitting needle, drawing the wool through at the same time; pass the bodkin through the next stitch as for purl, but do not slip the stitch from the knitting needle, only draw the wool through it. Purl the first stitch from the back needle, and draw the wool through at the same time, then knit the next stitch on the back needle plain, drawing the wool through but not slipping the stitch from the needle.

Return to the front needle and knit the next stitch off it, purl the next and leave it on; purl the next stitch from the back needle and knit the next one, leaving it on. Continue in this way until all the stitches have been worked off both needles, then fasten off securely. You will find that the two edges of knitting have been joined invisibly and there is no thickness, as would be caused if the two edges were sewn together. The stitches at the toe of a sock should always be grafted.

A BONNET FOR A BABY OR A LARGE DOLL

Work this bonnet in garter stitch or plain knitting. If it is required for a baby, the piece of knitting, when finished, should measure about 13 inches long and 10 or 12 inches deep. To make sure of a good fit, measure the doll or baby round the face and again from the forehead to the extreme back of the head. For a baby, add 2 inches to the back-to-front measurement—this allows a portion of the front of the bonnet to be turned back from the face.

You will not need more than two ounces of two-ply vest wool for a baby, and probably you will be able to manage with less than that quantity. Use bone needles No. 8. If needles and wool of these sizes are used, you may assume that seven stitches will measure 1 inch, and from this you may estimate the number of stitches needed to be cast on.

Begin at the front of the bonnet and cast on the number of stitches required according to the face measurement. Now knit backwards and forwards in plain knitting until you have made the work 2 inches deeper than the measurement from the back to the front of the head; there is no shaping to be done. When the size required has been completed, cast off the stitches and break off the wool.

The next thing is to sew up the back. Take a length of wool, thread it into a bodkin and run it along the edge where you cast off. Draw up this wool so that the work is gathered a little, but be careful not to draw it so tightly that it becomes bunchy. Now place the two corners together, find the middle of the back, and sew these two gathered portions together, from the corners to the middle, arranging the gathers as smoothly as possible; finish off neatly and flat. Choose some bébé ribbon to match the bonnet, thread it into a bodkin, run it in and out round the bottom of the bonnet.

Be careful to turn back the fronts so that the bonnet measures the right size from the back before you thread it with ribbon. This must be threaded in and out at equal distances all round the sides, while at each end of the turned back portions of the front, it must be passed through the two thicknesses of knitting, so that the fronts are kept in position. Cut the ribbon, leaving a long end at each corner of the front, to tie under the chin. Stitch the ribbon in place at the back so that it will not be drawn out accidentally.

A KNITTED COAT FOR A DOLL OR A BABY

If this coat is intended to be worn with the bonnet, described under the heading *A Bonnet for a Baby or a Large Doll*, it must be worked in garter stitch, to match. But if preferred, it may be worked in stocking stitch.

The diagram is intended to fit a medium sized baby of one year; if you measure your doll or baby, you will be able to estimate what alterations to make. The length across the back, length of sleeve, and the height from hem to neck will be the measurements needed. The diagram shows average proportions which must be increased or reduced as needed. As in the bonnet, you can assume that seven stitches measure one inch; this will help you to know how many stitches to cast on.

Start at the lower edge of the back (A, B) and cast on 84 stitches, if you are keeping to the size of the diagram. Knit garter stitch for 7½ inches. Now you must cast on for the sleeves. When you have knitted to the end of a row, do not break off the wool, but cast on as many stitches as will be needed for the length of the sleeve, probably 66 or 70. Turn the work and knit back over the cast on stitches, continue right across the back, and cast on an equal number of stitches for the other sleeve; turn the work and knit back to the other wrist. Work garter stitch for 3½ inches.

It is now necessary to leave a space for the neck. Count the total number of stitches on the needle, deduct 30 for the neck and divide the result by two. If you started with 84 and added 70 for each sleeve, the total on the needle will be 224. When you have deducted 30 for the neck, 194 will be left ; halve this and you have 97.

This is the way to make the neck hole ; knit the first 97 stitches on to a spare needle and keep them on it until they are needed again ; cast off the next 30 stitches for the neck, and knit the remaining 97. Turn the work and knit back to the neck. Cast on 20, and knit garter stitch on these (97+20) for 3½ inches. You have now finished one sleeve. Cast off the stitches which you added for the sleeve, then knit on the remainder for 7½ inches—that is, to the front bottom edge of the coat. Cast off all these stitches, and leave several inches of wool free, after you have broken it off.

For the other side of the front, cast on 20 stitches to one of the needles, and then, from the spare needle, knit the 97 stitches, adding them to the 20 which you have cast on. On these knit garter stitch for 3½ inches, for the second sleeve. Now cast off the 70 stitches which were added

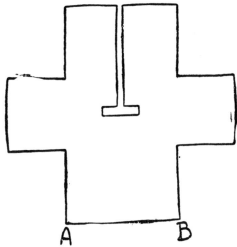

A   B

for the sleeve and knit garter stitch for 7½ inches on the remainder, and then cast off.

The cuffs must now be made. Pick up the stitches on the lower edge of the sleeve and knit about 1½ or 2 inches of moss stitch. Do this on both sleeves and cast off.

Before joining up the seams, press the coat on the wrong side, with a damp cloth between it and the iron. Sew up each sleeve seam on the wrong side, and continue down the under arm to the lower edge of the coat.

On each sleeve turn back the portions which you have knitted at the wrists, to act as cuffs.

Finish off by crocheting a simple edging round the neck, fronts, lower edge and cuffs. This may be made by working one double crochet, one chain, one double crochet, one chain, and so on, all round, for the first row. In the second, make three trebles into every second space between two double crochets. For these stitches, see section for Crochet.

H

Thread some narrow ribbon through the edging round the neck and leave the ends long enough to tie.

PASSE-PARTOUT FRAMING

Many delightful pictures may be obtained at no cost whatever, since covers of price lists, magazine covers, book wrappers, and other advertising matter often attain a high artistic level. If the walls of your bedroom are bare of pictures, why not frame some of these covers and wrappers? The work may be done by the *passe-partout* method easily and cheaply.

This method consists in pasting a picture on a suitable card, placing a sheet of glass over it, and binding the two together by means of gummed strips of paper. The glass may, of course, be purchased in the ordinary way at the local glazier's, but we have a sixpenny glass-cutter with which we shape odd pieces of glass left over from window-mending jobs. The binding strips are sold in rolls by photographic dealers. Various colours can be procured. Gold is useful for most coloured pictures which are bright and vivid. Slate and grey go well with pictures delicately tinted; while black suits almost any print.

The binding is, perhaps, a little fidgety, but, until the art is acquired, we shall find that three clips will hold the card, picture, and glass together while we are binding the fourth side. Do not wet the gummed side of the strips too freely; in fact, we prefer to coat them with photo-mountant rather than water.

Hang the pictures by means of a loop of thin string, or in the case of tiny pictures, of fine white cotton. Place the loop exactly in the centre of the top edge of the back. To find the centre, mark off the width of the back on a sheet of paper and fold it. This will give the length of half the back.

Small pictures may often be improved by mounting them on large white or grey sheets, which, in turn, are fixed to cards of the same size. When this is done, see that the margins at the sides are equal, that the space at the top is equal to or more than the sides, and that the bottom is obviously greater than the three other spaces.

A PORTABLE WRITING OUTFIT

Have you an old attaché case which has grown shabby, and the lock, probably gone wrong? If so, you might like to transform it into this portable writing outfit.

You will see from the illustration how the inside has to be fitted. There is a partition, behind which notepaper, envelopes, post-cards, and other every-day necessities are stored. In the front of the partition two or three pairs of loops are placed, to carry pencils, a fountain pen, etc. In addition, there is plenty of extra space for whatever other fittings and gadgets you consider necessary. The front flap is a blotting pad, when opened out.

In the illustration, the sides have been cut, so that they taper. This is merely done for effect and is not necessary. If you decide to trim your case in the same way, you must remember that the opening flap will, then, be too short to reach up to the edge that carries the handle.

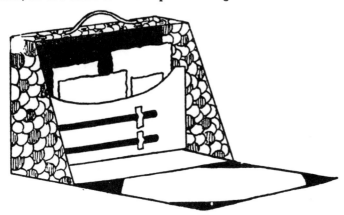

It must either be replaced by a flap slightly longer, or a strip of card may be glued along the sloping edge, at the top, to meet it.

Instead of a lock, the two ends of a neat strap are used; one end is stitched below the handle, and the other on the edge of the flap.

You will cover all the outer faces and the inside, including the partition, with some pretty cretonne, or, failing this, a smart wallpaper. Cretonne, it may be said, can be stuck with liquid glue, so long as a short time elapses between the spreading and the fixing.

PICTORIAL LETTER WRITING

Have you ever tried your hand at making a pictorial message? The game is quite easy if you can draw passably. Perhaps you have not quite grasped the idea. It is this: instead of writing words in the usual way, you draw pictures to represent the things you have to say. For instance, let us suppose that your message starts with the words "I hear you are not well." First you draw an eye. Then after a little space you print the letter H touching an ear. Following another short space comes a yew tree, or, if that is too hard to draw, the letter U standing by itself will do quite well. Next comes, in its proper spacing, the letter R, followed by a piece of string with a big knot in it. Lastly, a tiny well with the necessary top to it is drawn. This completes the short remark we selected above; but, of course, you will continue to much greater length.

Two cautions: spaces should separate each word, so that it is obvious where one begins and ends; do not use more letters than you can help.

A USEFUL PENWIPER

Cut the lengths of black wool to reach from the tip of the head to the lowest part of the feet. Tie up the body first, then slip through the chest the hank of wool serving for the arms. Tie the head, legs, etc., and sew on black boot buttons for the eyes. Make the mouth of white wool.

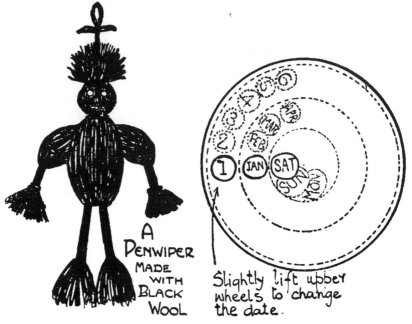

A Useful Penwiper   An Everlasting Calendar

AN EVERLASTING CALENDAR

Cut a circular card of, we will say, 6 inches in diameter. Lightly pencil the horizontal diameter. In the half of this diameter to the left of the centre, cut three circular holes, each about half an inch across. Make the first one, half an inch from the edge; the second, an inch and a quarter from the edge, and the third, two inches from the edge.

Now cut cards of the following diameters, (*a*) two and a quarter inches, (*b*) three and three-quarter inches, (*c*) five and a half inches. Place all the cards together in the following order, the six inch card on top and then *a*, *b* and *c*. Put a paper fastener through the centre of them all, and run it round a few times so that the holes are circular.

Through the holes in the top card, you can now see little portions of *a*, *b* and *c*. Take first of all the card we have called *c*. You can see a piece of it through the outer hole. In that space, neatly print the figure 1. Now, twist the circle so that one just disappears, then print the figure 2. Next, twist the circle so that the two disappears, then print the figure 3. Continue in this way up to 31.

Turn now to the card we have called *b*. You can see a small portion of it through the second hole. In that space, write "Jan." Then turn it on and in the blank space so obtained write "Feb." Follow with all the months of the year.

In the third hole, which belongs to card *a*, write the days of the week, from Sunday to Saturday—you can put Sun., Mon., Tues., and so on.

You now have a useful perpetual calendar. On the unused area of the top card, draw and paint some striking design, so that your contrivance is not only useful but ornamental as well.

A POSTCARD CASE

Everybody has to use postcards fairly frequently; accordingly, a case in which to keep supplies is a handy thing to have. To make such a case is not difficult. First, you will want two pieces of stout card, a trifle larger than an ordinary postcard, which is 5½ by 3½ inches. Thus, the two stout cards should be about 5¾ by 3¾ inches.

The next thing is to select a nice piece of silk or cretonne such as is used for covering chairs and cushions. Place the two cards with the short sides together, but with a space of 1½ inches separating them, both back and front, turn in the edges and sew up. It is advisable to run

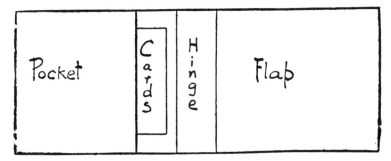

two rows of stitches where the cards end off, so that they cannot slip towards each other.

Now fold the contrivance in halves, and, when you have the outer points exactly over each other, press along the hinge with a warm iron.

The cover of the case is now made, but you still have to fashion the pocket. Take another piece of the silk or cretonne, about 4 inches square, turn in the edges and sew round three sides, and fix them to the inner face of one of the cover-flaps. This finishes the work.

Be careful to make the pocket sufficiently large to take a stack of about 25 cards, so do not put the material on too tightly. A good plan is to fit the pocket with some cards in position.

MAKING CHRISTMAS CARDS

There are dozens of ways of making splendid Christmas cards. Do not think that if you set to work and do them yourself, people will look upon them as makeshift articles. They will know that you took a good deal of trouble over them, and they will value them all the more. Also, you will save money by turning out your own cards.

Probably the best way to begin will be to procure a sheet of stout drawing paper. A two-penny sheet will serve for about a dozen cards. Now think of the envelopes that are at your disposal. It is no good making odd sized cards that will not fit any envelopes on earth. When you have decided this matter, begin to cut up some, not a lot, of the paper. The way to do it is to fold it and then cut with a paper knife. The slightly rough edge will appear as if it is deckled. Single sheets do not, as a rule, look well, but a folded sheet is usually satisfactory. Therefore cut your paper to twice the required size and then fold it. On the

first page, do the ornamental part, and on the third print the wording. Leave pages two and four blank.

Now, what are we to select by way of ornamentation for the front page? All sorts of ideas will probably occur to you. You may have kept the best of last year's cards. Why not get ideas from them? Or, look at some of the advertisements in the high-class magazines? Little designs or pictures form part of the announcements, and many will do admirably for your purpose. If you have an album in which your friends have done things, look through it and see if you can get an idea or two from their efforts. There is no doubt that, with a little thought, you will be able to draw up two or three really useful schemes.

More will be unnecessary, because there is no reason why many of the cards should not be alike.

If you decide on doing say six cards all alike, we should certainly advise you to trace the outline of all but the first. And, here is another tip. Most of your pictorial attempts will be enclosed in a rectangular frame. Cut a post-card to the exact size of the frame, then place the card just where you want the rectangle, and pencil guide lines around its edge. You can do a dozen frames accurately in five minutes in this way; but they would take considerably longer if each one had to be measured individually.

Roughly speaking, the chosen design will take one of three forms. The first will be a water-colour drawing, the second a pen and ink sketch, and the third a combination of the two former types. The first should only be attempted if you are good at this class of work. You must know how to put colours on without streaks, how to blend colours, and how to avoid going over the edges with the paint. It is not a very easy business, and you will have to be something of an artist.

The second class of work is easier. You can usually trace the outlines and ink them in after. Never use ordinary writing ink; it looks poor and shabby for sketches. Indian ink gives a much better effect. Have an ordinary nib for the heavy lines, and a fine mapping pen for the lighter ones. If all the work is done with a thick nib, it will look clumsy.

The third class, where sketching is combined with colour work, is perhaps the most effective of all. In this case, use Indian ink, as before, but see that it is fixed ink. It costs no more and it will not run. Remember that washes of colour should never be put on top of large patches of ink, but it will not matter if colour is painted over fine ink lines.

We have given three specimen cards among the illustrations. The first is easily done. In black, it does not perhaps appear very effective, but if the printing is black, the leaves and pot are green, and the berries red, then it becomes quite smart. Of course, you can alter the wording to suit your individual friends, and there need be nothing written on the third page.

The second illustration is just a funny little sketch of a cheeky nature. Do the mistletoe in green, the face and wording in black, but just touch up the cheeks in red.

The third illustration shows the three wise men. It is a silhouette picture, and, let it be said, silhouettes are very easy to do, as a mistake in a line can usually be rectified without showing. This design looks very effective, if the dark clouds in the sky are done in a heavy grey-blue and the lighter clouds in grey. Just over the buildings, the grey should merge into a golden hue.

Do not forget, when posting your cards, that a half-penny stamp will be correct for any place inland, if the flap of the envelope is not stuck down. Three-half-pence is the charge when the envelope is closed.

A CHRISTMAS TREE

Christmas only comes once a year, unfortunately, but if the weather is cold or rainy and you must play indoors, why not have a Christmas tree? Get a piece of cardboard about 18 inches high and 9 inches wide. An old cardboard box lying empty and discarded in the attic will suit nicely. Draw on it in pencil the outline of a tree in a pot, something like the one in the diagram. Colour the tree a vivid green and the pot a jolly pillar-box red, and then cut out the shape. Our tree must stand up, so shape out another piece of card, as shown in B, and fix it behind the pot by means of two small paper clips.

Now a tree is not a Christmas tree until it is loaded with toys, so we must lose no time in hanging all sorts of attractive things on our tree. But how and what ? Get a sheet of white paper, and on it draw, colour and cut out some tiny dolls, balls, crackers, boxes of tin trains, boxes of sweets, stockings, books, and miniature pictures of the presents you had

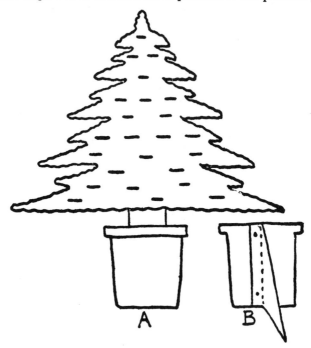

A   B

last year. When cutting out the things, leave a little white tab at the top of each, a quarter of an inch wide and an inch long. Now make a number of little slits all over the tree, half an inch wide. All that now remains is to push the tabs into the slits, and your tree becomes gaily decorated with all manner of Christmas presents in miniature.

DECORATING CANDLES

There has been a great vogue, in recent years, for decorated candles. They add an attractive note to the supper-table, when a little party is being given, to the bedroom mantelpiece and dressing-table, and the uses to which they are put in churches should not be overlooked.

There is nothing difficult about transforming an ordinary cheap candle into one of rare beauty. For preference, select one of fair length, as the short specimens do not show off your decorative work to the best advantage.

First, hold the candle by the wick and give it an even coat of spirit varnish. This will dry in a short time. Then, follow with a coat of white of egg, to which has been added about half as much warm water. Next, paint those parts of the design that are intended to be gilt with gold-size and, when it has become tacky, cover over with gold leaf, by dabbing it on. Then, leave the work for twenty-four hours ; at the end of this time, the other colours may be worked up.

Note that if gold-paint instead of gold-leaf is used, you may omit the application of gold-size. Also, if gold does not enter into the scheme of decoration, the candle should be varnished as already mentioned, but the coat of egg-water is not given.

The colours needed for candle-painting are ground in oils, such as dealers of artists' materials sell in small tubes. They should be mixed

with copal varnish rather than turpentine to thin them to a proper working consistency. When the paints have dried, it is advisable, though not necessary, to give them a covering of mastic varnish. When this is hard, they are then ready for use.

The paints may be applied in any manner that appears convenient, but we have found that, by propping up the tip of the candle on a small cushion or a heap of rags and letting the far end rest on the table, the candle assumes a convenient angle at which to work. A bridge for supporting the hand is, then, erected over the candle. This is formed by two stacks of books or boxes, with a strip of wood across them. (See the diagram.)

Probably, you will have your own ideas as to what is a suitable design for a first attempt. Perhaps we may say that spiral bands of colour look very neat and are not at all difficult to do well.

PAPER HATS

Lots of fun can be had out of paper hats. If you want to make a few for a party, or, may be, for your little regiment of make-believe soldiers, this is the way to do it.

Get some large sheets of paper. Newspaper is hardly stout enough ; brown paper is much better ; but why not hunt out some gay-coloured papers—reds, blues, greens, etc. ? Let each sheet be not quite square— say a quarter more one side than the other, as Diagran A. Now fold as follows :

I

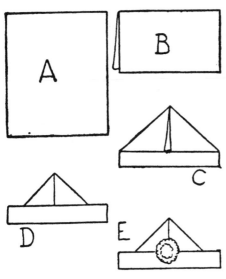

(1) Halve the long edges and double the paper over so that the crease joins the two half-way points, as Diagram B.

(2) Bend over the two upper corners so that they meet down the middle, as Diagram C.

(3) Fold the lower edges so that they double over the triangular top, one at the front and one at the back, as Diagram D. The hat can now be opened out and worn.

It makes a nice addition if the hats are ornamented by having coloured rosettes or other gay decorations pasted on to them. The rosette shown in Diagram E not only serves as a splendid ornamentation, but it helps to keep the hat from coming undone.

A LUGGAGE LABEL

A waterproof luggage label is a necessity for the globe-trotter, being far more secure and much neater than the paper variety.

To make one of these labels, cut two rectangles of American cloth, each about 4 by 2½ inches. If your cases are green, purple, plum-coloured, etc., choose cloth to match; otherwise, use black material. Then take the two pieces, round off two adjacent corners and cut a triangle off each of the other two corners. The diagram shows exactly what is required.

When this is done, make a slit in each piece of the cloth, as shown at A, and a large rectangle in one piece only, as shown at B.

The next step is to bind the two panels together. This is done by piercing small holes with a fine awl and sewing through them with strong carpet thread. Note, however, that the two pieces of American cloth must not be completely closed up by the sewing. A gap should be left for the insertion of a stout card, bearing the name and address. Therefore, begin where the upper cross indicates, work to the right and go round the edges to the lower cross. For the sake of appearance, you may continue the stitching from the lower cross to the upper one, but only bind the edges of the top piece of cloth, *i.e.*, the one that serves as the face side of the label.

The last step is to obtain a small buckle, to cut a strap of thin leather, about 8 inches long—a piece of an old watch-strap will do nicely—and to thread it through the two slots marked A; then, to fit one end of the strap over the shank of the buckle and sew the two thicknesses together. The rest of the fitting is too obvious to need any further description.

If possible, secure a sheet of the transparent material, such as is used in season-ticket cases, and let it lie on top of the card, bearing the name and address, so that it acts as a protection against wet and rain.

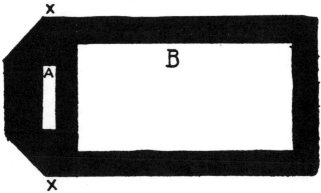

It may be added that much the best material we know of for the label itself, that is the white strip on which the name and address is written, is a piece cut out of an old stiff white collar. Probably, your father or your brother can supply you with one or two collars which have come back from the laundry in such a condition that they are past wearing. Instead of throwing them away, they will be just the thing for your purpose.

A TRAVELLER'S WASHING COMPENDIUM

The worst of travelling, especially by train or car, is that one becomes dirty so quickly, and, once the feeling of being untidy and begrimed is experienced, it is " good-bye " to comfort, until an opportunity to wash occurs.

With a washing compendium in your pocket, there is seldom any need to feel dirty, because water can be, usually, obtained, and the compendium supplies all the other requisites.

This little outfit consists of (1) a towel, which rolls up into a small space, (2) a miniature cake of soap, wrapped in a cover of waterproof sheeting, (3) a small face-glove, (4) a pocket-comb, and (5) a tiny mirror.

These items are arranged as follows : the towel is folded into three or four, making a long strip, about 5 inches wide. Then the other articles are placed within the folds, as the strip is rolled up. In this manner the whole equipment takes up very little space, but, naturally, it requires some outer covering. This can be made from a choice of materials, such as a piece of waterproof, glazed American cloth, or thin supple leather, lined with waterproof.

We will describe, here, how to make this compendium case of leather, lined with waterproof, leaving you to recognise for yourself how to set about the work, if you decide on the easier plan of using a single thickness of American cloth or waterproof sheeting.

Seek out a piece of leather, 12 inches long and 6 inches wide, and a piece of thin waterproof sheeting of the same dimensions. Place the leather flat on the work-table, face side down, and the sheeting on top of it, face side up. Then fold over the two thicknesses to the extent of four inches and sew along two parallel sides. When making the stitches, be very careful to see that they take in the sheeting as well as the leather. In this way, the pocket is formed.

All that is necessary to do to the flap is to turn in the raw edges of the waterproof, and to sew, neatly, around the three edges of the two thicknesses. The leather may be left with a raw edge, if it has been carefully cut in the first place.

One or two little matters remain for consideration. The edge of the pouch must be sewn, in order to join the sheeting to the leather. Also, some people will prefer to make the stitches where they will be out of sight. This will be especially the case when American cloth or a single piece of waterproof is used. For this, the material must be folded in a contrary sense to that mentioned above; then the pouch is turned inside out when it has been sewn.

Some form of fastening arrangement is needed. Press-studs will, naturally, suggest themselves, but as the contents of the bag are of a soft pliant nature, it is not an easy matter to snap them. In this case, therefore, it will be better to sew an elastic loop at the back of the bag, and by stretching it slightly, it can be made to slip entirely round the pouch and close it effectively.

The washing compendium makes an admirable birthday gift for a friend, and it will sell well at a bazaar. If three or four are made of the same materials, it is possible to average out the cost of each at about one and six to two shillings, including the contents, and they would sell readily at three-and-six or four shillings.

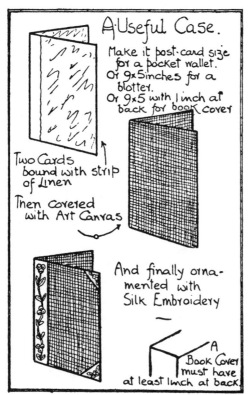

A Useful Case.

Make it post-card size for a pocket wallet. Or 9x5 inches for a blotter. Or 9x5 with 1 inch at back for book cover

Two Cards bound with strip of Linen

Then Covered with Art Canvas

And finally orna-mented with Silk Embroidery

A
Book Cover must have at least 1 inch at back.

USEFUL FANCY CASES

These illustrations offer some useful suggestions for pocket cases and book covers of a fancy nature.

They are easy to make and are constructed with odd pieces of material such as are found in almost every home. For sticking the materials, any thick paste or tube glue is advised.

A BOTTLE-WRAP FOR TRAVELLERS

When you pack your week-end bag, there are always two or three bottles that have to be stowed carefully where they are least likely to be broken. As a matter of fact, they are a nuisance ; but they are, nevertheless, necessary and cannot be left out, so in they must go.

Here is a very brainy idea. It enables you to carry a bottle without any fear of breakage and it is very easy to make. Moreover, it is pretty, and gives a neat appearance to your belongings.

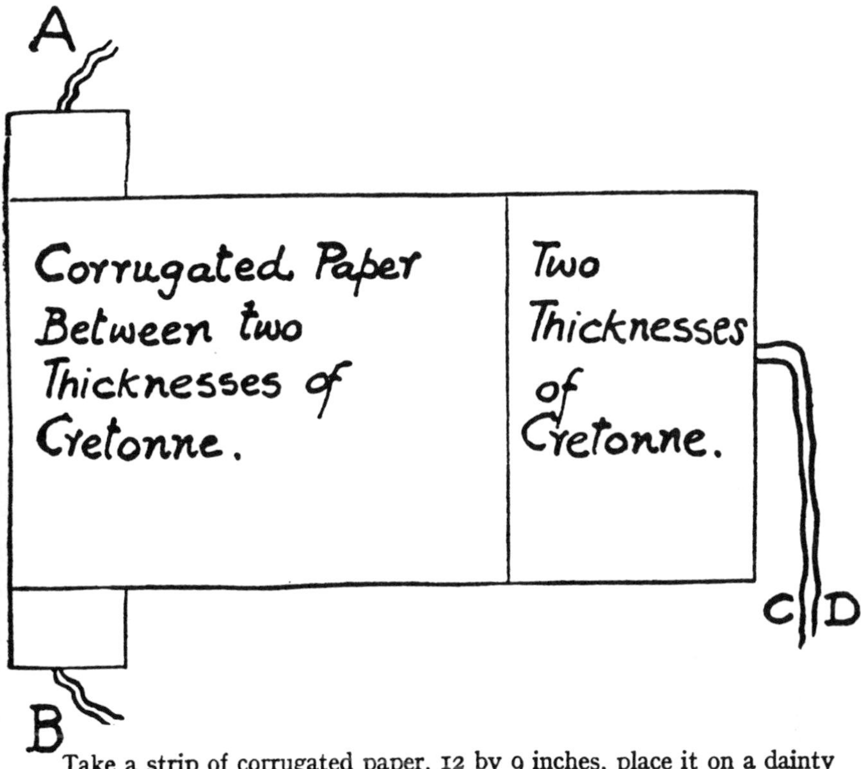

A

Corrugated Paper
Between two
Thicknesses of
Cretonne.

Two
Thicknesses
of
Cretonne.

C D

B

Take a strip of corrugated paper, 12 by 9 inches, place it on a dainty piece of cretonne, 19 by 19 inches, fold over the cretonne and sew all round the edges. To make this quite clear, refer to the diagram. There you will see that the final shape measures 18 inches long by 9 inches wide. Two-thirds of its length are composed of corrugated paper, sandwiched between two thicknesses of cretonne, while the remaining third is merely a double thickness of cretonne, without any corrugated paper.

The next step is to sew on two flaps of the same cretonne, double thickness, in the positions indicated in the diagram, and to fix a length of ribbon, as shown at A and B. Finally, two more strips of ribbon are sewn at C and D.

To use this sensible contrivance, place the bottle on the main strip of the envelope, lengthwise between the two flaps ; then, fold over the flaps and tie A and B in a bow. Roll up the envelope, commencing at the left and proceeding to the right. When it is all wound round the bottle, tie the ribbons, C and D.

The dimensions given here are suitable for a medicine bottle, or any other bottle of approximately the same size.

A little while ago, we made a number of articles for a bazaar. Half a dozen of these bottle-wraps were among the items. They were all sold within ten minutes of the opening. So if you want a good notion for your next sale of work or bazaar we advise you to remember this useful contrivance.

SLIPPERS MADE OF FELT

Felt is a very cosy material for bedroom slippers. If you would like to make a pair of these useful articles, first purchase two fleecy-covered soles for threepence or sixpence, but get them a size larger than the shoe usually worn. Then build up the slippers around them.

We have drawn a slipper, as a guide, but any slight deviation from the shape may be easily made, if desired. Two inset drawings show

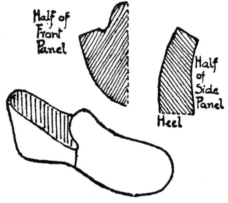

how the front panel is to be formed, and, similarly, with the portion that runs from the instep, round the back of the heel to the other side. To shape these pieces, fold the material and cut two thicknesses in one. For the purpose, select some gay-coloured felt, but do not have it too heavy.

In building up the slippers, begin at the toe and work both ways from it. When the front panel is attached, turn to the side piece and sew that, first to the front panel and then to the sole. The seam down the instep is the only part that overlaps ; nowhere else should the material be folded over, as it is too thick. All the raw edges are finished by an oversewn stitch.

It is not possible to give the exact measurements for the various pieces, as shoes and slippers vary so much in size. Your best plan is to take one of your shoes, measure it, and make slight extra allowances for stitching. If you have been too generous, it is always possible to trim away small pieces as you proceed.

When the slippers have been built up, it is not a bad plan to decorate the fronts with coloured wools, or to sew on each a shaped piece of some other bright material.

A PAPER DRINKING CUP

Take a piece of grease-proof paper, about 8 inches square (Fig. 1) and fold it along the diameter, so that it makes two triangles (see figure 2).

Then fold the left-hand side of the triangle, so that it resembles figure 3, and follow with the right-hand side of the triangle, making it like figure 4. Next, bend over the top points, to look like figure 5. There are two top points, one behind the other. They are not folded over together, but away from each other, one on either side.

Now, bulge the sides and you have a small drinking cup, which will prove very useful at picnics and at other makeshift meals.

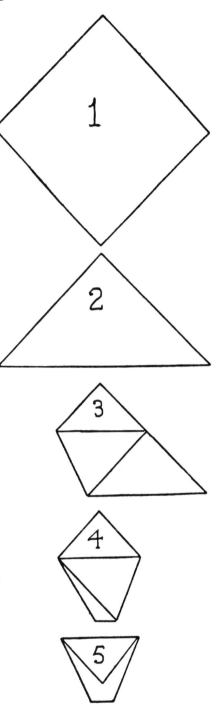

HOW TO MAKE THINGS IN RAFFIA

The number and variety of things which may be made or embroidered with raffia is surprising. The work is easy and quick, and the materials required are not expensive. A small girl need only save a little of her pocket-money for a week or two, then she can buy a few bundles of raffia and a small piece of canvas, and with it make a most charming present for her mother. A hat ornament, a needle-case, a shopping-bag, or a pochette, can all be made for less than two shillings.

Several kinds of coloured raffia may be bought. The cheapest is in bundles which cost about two shillings a pound. It is usually necessary to wind this kind, and sometimes even to split it, as the widths are not regular. The most convenient way is to procure it in balls, at about threepence each. There is then no need to wind it, there is no waste and no muddle.

It is impossible to avoid a mess when a large hank has to be sorted and wound ; and if it is not wound, but taken from the hank when required, it very soon becomes tangled. These small balls may be pur-chased at most oil and colour merchants, while larger balls of the same quality are usually to be obtained from art needlework shops. For very dainty work, it is advisable to buy artificial silk raffia at a slightly higher cost.

In addition to the raffia you will need a packet of chenille needles. These are rather like darning needles, but not so long, and have a very large eye and a blunt point.

The actual embroidery may be done on any canvas or straw articles which you may already possess, such as a plain waste paper basket, a canvas shopping bag or a coarse straw hat.

If, however, you prefer to make something which is entirely your own handiwork, you will have to buy some canvas for making up and embroidering. There are many degrees of coarseness to be obtained. A fine one is apt to split the threads of raffia, so it is advisable to avoid that variety ; a coarse one will require more work in order to cover the threads satisfactorily. Therefore a medium one is best. It costs about 2s. 3d. a yard, but a quarter of a yard is sufficient for a pochette handbag ; so it is not expensive.

It is possible to buy the canvas shape for a handbag with a coloured design already printed on it. If you intend to use one of these, you will find it more expensive than buying the plain canvas which you cut out yourself ; but the actual working will be simpler, as the colours in the design will be a guide as to how they should be arranged, and you will therefore not be troubled with the question of working out a pattern or colour scheme yourself.

A RAFFIA-EMBROIDERED NEEDLE CASE

For this little case you will require a piece of canvas 4 inches by 6 inches ; some gold paint ; brightly coloured raffia of various shades; ribbon, about 1 inch wide for binding the edges; a small piece of silk or wide ribbon for lining, and some white flannel.

Cut the canvas roughly to the above-mentioned dimensions, then paint it on both sides with the gilt paint, being careful not to miss the corners of the mesh of the canvas. When it has been allowed to dry thoroughly, see that the edges are quite straight, and trim them, where necessary; then fold it by placing the two shorter sides together. You now have a book-shaped cover. In the centre of one of the sides work a spray of small flowers and leaves, with the raffia. The petals of the flowers are formed by making one chain stitch for each petal; make four or five to each flower and finish off the centre with a cluster of French knots of a contrasting colour. Leaves are represented by long straight stitches of green raffia. Work several flowers of various colours and a few leaves, arranging them in a spray or bunch.

Place the ribbon or silk selected for the lining on the wrong side of the embroidered canvas and oversew it to the four sides. Bind these sides with the narrow ribbon, hemming along both its edges very neatly.

Cut two pieces of flannel rather smaller than the canvas, and scallop round the edges with a pair of scissors; place these one above the other on the canvas, and stitch them all firmly together along the centre fold.

You now have a little book, the pages being of flannel and the covers of gilt canvas. Stick a few pins and needles in these pages, and sew a short length of narrow ribbon to the centre of each edge, opposite the fold of the book; these can be tied in a bow when the case is not in use.

A RAFFIA SHOPPING BAG

Perhaps you would like to make a bag entirely yourself, either for a present to somebody or in which to keep your shoes, or needlework. Why not make one entirely of raffia? It will not be expensive and will not take long to make.

You will need two pieces of canvas of the same size, one for each side of the bag; several balls of brightly coloured raffia, a chenille needle, and some material for lining.

K

First of all decide on the size and shape of the bag and then cut out the two sides. Now work out a simple design, and with a pencil, lightly draw it on the canvas. You will find no trouble in keeping it regular if you count the threads or spaces, while if you restrict yourself to squares, triangles or diamond shapes, you will have no difficulty in drawing and working a pattern.

The design need not fill the whole piece of canvas; a wide border of simple stitches might be worked for 3 or more inches round each edge of the bag; the centre ornament can take the form of a square or oblong, while the space between the border and design may be filled in with a fancy raffia stitch of a contrasting shade.

The centre design must be worked first. For this choose your colours carefully, having first decided what shade to make the border and the surround of fancy stitching.

If the centre pattern is composed of squares, try to arrange them so that the strands in each adjacent square are worked in different directions, not parallel to each other. This shows up the pattern more. Adjacent triangles, also, should have their stitches perpendicular, not parallel, to each other.

When you have worked a conspicuous design of a fair size, the surround may be added. A good idea is to work round and round the centre piece. Use a colour which will show up well against those already used, and beginning at the top left-hand corner of the centre pattern, work a solid square over five or six threads of the canvas, making the stitches vertical. Count the number of spaces you cover in this square, and make the same number of vertical stitches, side by side, as spaces covered, so that a square is formed. Next to this work another square, just the same size, but with the threads going horizontally; work the first horizontal stitch from the last top hole of the previous square, and make the next from the hole beneath, and so on.

Work alternately vertical and horizontal squares all round the centre decoration. Surround this with two or three more bands of squares of the same size, using another colour if desired, or keeping the same colour throughout ; place a vertical square over a horizontal one, and *vice versa*. When enough of this surround has been done, the final border may be worked right up to the outside edges of the canvas. Begin this, in another colour, at the top left-hand corner of the canvas, and make two vertical stitches, side by side, and of the same length, a space or two longer than those used for the solid squares of the surround.

The next two stitches, of the same size as the first, are worked beside the first two, but start two spaces lower down. The next two begin on a level with the first two, the fourth two, level with the second two, and so on. The next row is worked in the same way, each pair of stitches starting from the spaces at the base of the corresponding two in the previous row. Continue in this way until you reach the top row of the surround, when the stitches must be shortened, if necessary, to fit. Work down each side of the centre pattern and continue along the base of it, shortening the stitches if necessary in the first row below the design ; continue until the bottom edge of the canvas is reached. Fill in all spaces which are left at the top and bottom rows, with short stitches.

When the whole of this piece of canvas has been covered with raffia, the other piece must be done also. Both sides may be exactly alike, if desired, or a slightly different pattern may be used for the centres. Also it may be varied by using the same pattern on both, but by arranging the colours differently.

These sides being completed, it is now necessary to join them together. This is quite a simple matter. Turn in the frayed canvas all round, place the two pieces together, the wrong sides facing each other, but be careful that both the patterns are the right way up. Thread a chenille needle with raffia of a colour to tone with the rest of the bag—black, however, will look as well as any colour—and oversew them together with big stitches, working them as closely together as possible. Sew round the two sides and base of the bag, but not round the top.

Now take the two pieces of lining material, either sateen, silk or linen, place the right sides facing, and sew them together round the two sides and base ; then slip it inside the canvas bag, turn in the top edges neatly, and oversew it to the top edges of the canvas with the same shade of raffia as was used to join the sides.

Take several strands of raffia of every shade that has been used, and make with them a thick plait to serve as a handle. Sew this *very securely* to each side of the bag, not quite at the ends of the plait, but an inch or two away. When you are sure that it is quite firmly attached, unravel the ends of the handle and bunch them to look like tassels.

A WASTE-PAPER BASKET ORNAMENTED WITH RAFFIA

A really handsome present suitable for a Christmas or birthday gift can be made by colouring a plain waste-paper basket and decorating it with raffia.

The baskets are not expensive to buy ; they may be painted with hat dyes any colour you like, or, if you want a particularly ornate affair, a small bottle of gold paint, applied very carefully with a fine brush, will produce a most attractive basket.

Allow plenty of time for the paint or dye to dry thoroughly before you begin to work with the raffia. Decide what kind of design you would like to work. You may elect to use some of the patterns described elsewhere for other raffia articles, such as large daisies and long green leaves. These flowers may be worked in any colour with contrasting colours for the centres. Or you may prefer to decorate the basket with a bunch of several different kinds of flowers.

Lightly outline the design in pencil first, in order to see exactly how the flowers and leaves should be arranged, and then work them. Large daisies (page 73) have already been described. A different type of daisy may be made by having a very much larger centre of brown or deep

yellow, with the petals considerably shorter than those of the larger variety ; arrange these petals very close together and overlapping.

A bunch of berries might also be introduced, to add a touch of scarlet ; also, a double rose could be made as follows :

Arrange a small space to be filled in later for the centre and round this work three stitches to form a triangle. Start the next stitch behind one side of the triangle at the centre of it ; loop the raffia loosely round the point of the triangle and pass the needle down half-way behind the second side of the triangle. Do not draw these stitches tightly, but ease them a little so that they may look like turned back petals. Do two or three more layers, starting each mid-way behind the previous row and over-lapping them at the corners. When the rose is large enough, fill the space at the centre with a tight mass of short yellow stitches or tiny loops.

The ornamentation may be arranged as a solid mass of blooms at one side of the basket, or as a deep band going all round it a few inches from the top.

A DINNER MAT IN RAFFIA

One of the first things to make with raffia is a table mat, suitable for putting hot dishes on. Cut out an oval of cardboard and remove a central oval, as shown in Diagram A, p. 78. The edge of the cut-out part should be as nearly parallel as possible. Of course, you will make the mat a little larger than the dishes with which it is to be used. Take a suitable shade of raffia, say green, red, or biscuit colour, and commence the winding as shown in Diagram A. Use a good long strip, because joins should be avoided as much as possible. Wind the material tightly, or it will slip and look unbusiness-like. Always place each wind in such a position that it overlaps half of the previous wind. This is necessary, because the raffia shrinks on drying, and, if the winds are laid side by side, there will be gaps when it is dry and the card support will show.

When a strand of raffia is nearly finished, commence with a new strand on the underside, as shown in Diagram A, then finish the old strand and tuck the loose end under at least two tight strands. Diagram B shows the completed mat.

After you have made an oval mat, you may care to make two or three round ones on the same lines.

A SHOPPING BASKET IN COLOURED RUSH

With coloured rush, quite a number of useful articles can be contrived. In the first case, long lengths of rush are made by plaiting three-ply strands, as described above. These are then taken and sewn into a suitable shape. If it is desired to make a shopping bag, sew the plaits into one large circle, 18 inches in diameter, and also two small ones, 5 inches in diameter.

These three pieces are shaped into a bag by taking the large circle and creasing it, as shown at E, and then fitting in a small circle at each end, to provide the shape shown at F, in the illustration on page 78. Lengths of the plait are used for making the handles.

All the sewing mentioned for this bag is done with thin twine. Many people use thread, but it is hardly strong enough. The stitches should be run through the material on the wrong side and not merely through the angles of the plait. In this way, they will hold well and they will not drag much.

The colour scheme for such a bag as this offers a good deal of scope, if you are artistically inclined. Biscuit-coloured rush is, probably, the best kind to use, but rings and edgings of red, green and blue material will add a lively touch. They may be provided by working in plaits of appropriate colours at the correct point in the stitching. The correct point is, however, not at all easy to gauge, and we prefer to make up the whole body of the bag with biscuit rush, and then paint the rings we want, tinting with red or green ink, or a suitable blue hat dye. With a little care, and by not being over generous with the colours, very pleasing effects are obtained.

A PIN-CUSHION IN RAFFIA

This useful little article is made in exactly the same way as the serviette ring, just described; but when the ring is complete, a cushion is made to fit the ring. It is forced into the opening and stitched in position. Use soft rag for the stuffing of the cushion and a nice piece of silk for the top covering. The top should be plumped up into a dome shape.

A SERVIETTE RING IN RAFFIA

Here is another pretty thing to make in raffia. Cut a ring, 1½ inches wide, from a cardboard tube or roll, and see that the edges are nice and smooth. Now begin the winding, as mentioned above, and continue until the cardboard is completely covered. Make each wind overlap a good deal, because the more it is lapped the flatter will the material lie. Diagram C shows the finished ring.

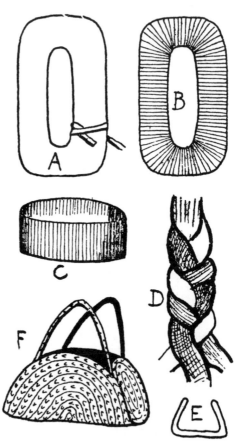

A variation of the method is provided by using plaited strands instead of flat ones. Take nine strands of the raffia, and, using three strands at a time, make a three-way plait (Fig. D). When a long length has been plaited tightly, flatten the length by pressing lightly with a cold iron. Then use the length for covering the cardboard ring. Overlap as much as possible ; but this is not so easy with the plaits as with the flat material. If the length is not long enough to cover the ring, more must be plaited on to it to make it sufficiently long. A new plait would cause an unwanted join. As you will see, this method allows you to use a variety of coloured strands, which will provide a pleasing effect.

A WOOLLEN ENVELOPE-BAG

You probably have stowed away somewhere a box full of brightly coloured wools and silks.

With the aid of a piece of canvas—the kind which is used for raffia work—and a supply of material for working a pattern on it, a very pretty bag may be made.

From your stock of wools and silks, select a quantity of the most pleasing colours, and on the canvas, work a section, in order to estimate the quantity of wool which will be required to cover the bag. By doing this you will be able to get an idea as to how much more of any special colour you will require to buy ; or you may, perhaps, be lucky enough to have sufficient in hand.

Many kinds of designs may be worked on this canvas, but personally, we prefer geometrical patterns or straight lines of bright colour. When the size of the bag has been decided on, and the canvas has been cut out to the desired size, turn in all the edges to a width of half an inch and tack them down. The last step in the decoration of the canvas is made by stitching a plain edging over these turned-in sides. But do not attempt this until everything else is done, as constant handling may spoil the appearance of the border before the rest of the work has been completed.

A large-eyed, blunt-tipped needle, similar to those used for raffia work, is needed for working the wool. Thread a long strand into the needle and insert it through a hole at the top left-hand corner of the canvas, drawing it through from the underneath to the top. Do not start at the first row of holes below the turned in edge, but at the third or fourth row down, according to the length of stitches required for the design you intend to work.

When you have drawn the wool through to the right side, pass the needle down again through the hole immediately below the turned in edge, and in a vertical line directly above the hole through which the wool was drawn up. Then miss one row of vertical holes and repeat the stitch, *i.e.*, bring the needle from below to the right side through the hole in the third or fourth row from the edge, then pass the needle downwards again through the corresponding hole in the top row. Continue to do this until the further side of the bag is reached.

Now with another shade of wool, fill in the gaps between each stitch of the first row in exactly the same way, but instead of passing the wool up through the holes in the same horizontal lines as the first shade of wool, begin two holes down and draw the wool up through the second hole from the left and two holes below the first row ; then pass it down again through the hole which is three or four vertically above ; this leaves a small space uncovered below the turned in edge ; this row of spaces must be filled in with another shade of wool.

Start each row three or four holes below the previous row and in a contrasting colour ; continue until the entire piece of canvas has been covered.

If it is desired to add a motif of some kind to the decoration, it should be worked on the portion of the canvas which is intended for the front flap of the bag. Fill this design in with a shade of wool which will show up well, before the background is worked. When, in filling in the background, you eventually reach the design, you must graduate your stitches round it so that they do not overlap the outlines of the motif. Start each row of background, as usual, and finish as usual, leaving gaps and shortening stitches when you come to the design.

When all the canvas has been covered, it will be necessary to finish the edge all round. Select a wool of a shade which will contrast well with the rest of the colour scheme, and starting at the left-hand corner of one edge, work over and over this double thickness of canvas. Pass the wool from the right side through to the underneath, working in the holes which actually touch the edges of the covering design. Do not

miss any holes in the canvas, but work as closely as possible so that a firm tidy edge is produced. When a corner is reached, work several stitches over and over in each direction in order that the corners of the canvas may not peep through. The ornamentation of the bag will be completed when all the four edges have been covered with wool.

It is now necessary to line the bag. This is a simple matter ; from a piece of silk or velveteen cut a portion of exactly the same shape and size as the worked canvas ; turn in all the edges and hem them carefully to the sides of the decorated canvas, thus hiding all the knots and ends of wool.

The bag, as it now is, merely appears to be a flat oblong of material. Divide this, along its greatest width, into three equal portions, turn the first third over, so that the lining on each portion faces the other, and stitch the two sides of it neatly to the sides of the centre third. Leave the last section free. This should be the flap, ornamented with a motif, if one has been added. The two sections which are sewn together form a pouche, while the third portion is the flap, which may be merely folded over and left free, or, if preferred, it may be made to fasten by securing strong press studs to the centre of the front edge, on the inside, and to the corresponding place in the part of the canvas which forms the envelope.

A WARDROBE FOR YOUR BEDROOM

We have often heard it said that girls cannot do carpentry ; but we do not agree with this. Several of our acquaintances have made some very useful things. One of them recently constructed a wardrobe, and,

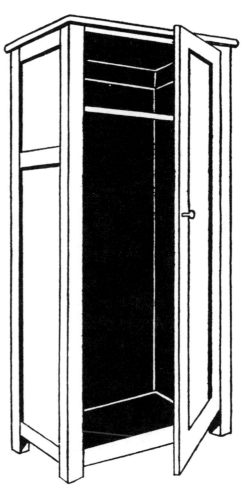

as it appeared to be a particularly complicated job, though, in reality, it was quite simple — we jotted down the details and offer them to other handy girls, who might like to make a similar wardrobe for themselves.

The diagram shows just what the cabinet looked like, and an examination of the various parts will save a good deal of verbal explanation.

The height is 6 feet ; the width 2½ feet, and the depth 2 feet. The last two dimensions may have to be varied, so that the cabinet can stand in a particular recess.

The four corner uprights are made of posts, 2½ inches square, and the same wood serves for the various horizontal pieces of the frame work.

It is advisable to make the two sides first ; then to fix the four horizontal pieces that separate the two sides, and to follow by putting on the back, the top, and the floor.

For the last three items, three-ply wood should be used and sheets of the same material serve for filling in the sides.

Screws or nails that are driven in from the outside, and are likely to show when the work is finished, are sunk below the surface, and the heads covered over with a dab of plastic wood. Thus, they are hidden from view.

A finish of dark oak stain was given in the case of the wardrobe which we have in mind, but paint or enamel are equally good.

The door is made of a frame of 2½ by 2 material, and filled in with a sheet of three-ply. It is in making this part of the wardrobe that the

L

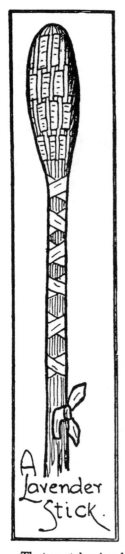

A
Lavender
Stick.

greatest difficulty will be experienced, and, rather than spoil the job, we suggest that a rod should be fixed where the opening comes, and a hanging curtain used instead of the door. That is, if the handy girl does not feel equal to making a good substantial door.

A LAVENDER STICK

Here is an unusual variation of the ordinary lavender sachet.

Take 24 sprigs of freshly gathered lavender and secure them in a tight bunch by winding strong sewing cotton round the top of the stalks, just below the blooms, so that all the heads are gathered together at the same level. Just below the cotton, bend up the stalks, taking care not to break them off, so that they surround the heads.

Take about 3 yards of soft purple bébé ribbon and gently thread it in and out among the stalks, starting at the bend of the stalks and winding it round so that the whole head is encased in a kind of lattice made of the stalks and ribbon. Draw the ribbon tightly as you proceed. Cut the stalks to an even length and wind the ribbon firmly round them to keep them together. When the end of the stalks is reached, fasten the ribbon securely and tie in a neat bow.

PRETTY BOXES AND HOW TO STORE THEM

If we had a dozen wardrobes and chests of drawers, we believe that there would always be an overflow of things which would have to be kept in large, shallow dress boxes. In fact, it seems that such boxes are indispensable.

That part having been explained, the next thing is to determine how the boxes are to be stored. To pile them up in a corner of the bedroom is to court untidiness, so this is what we have done. Fortunately for us, there is a recess in our bedroom which previously, was only tenanted by a chair. The chair was moved away and we took two pieces of wood, 3 feet high and as wide as the depth of the recess.

The wood was put flat on the concrete floor of the back yard and narrow strips, 1 inch square in section, were nailed horizontally across it, with roughly 7 inches between them. Having done this, the two pieces were taken to the recess in the bedroom, stood close up against the wall, facing each other, and shelves were wedged tightly between the strips so that they bedded on to the projecting strips.   A further piece of wood was wedged in, to serve as a top and this, be careful to note, had to be slightly larger than the shelves, because it fitted over to the edges of the first pieces.   This top was carefully smoothed with glasspaper

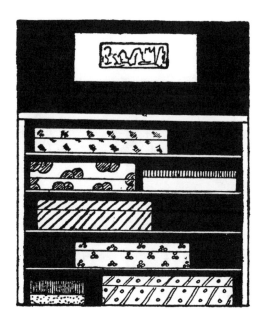

and painted white, because the room is white.   Lastly a cretonne curtain hangs in front of the shelves and hides the boxes from view.

Here, we have room for several large boxes, each containing a dress or something of the kind.   What we should do without this easily-made erection, we do not know.   One thing we do know—that is, dresses crease far less in these boxes than when rammed together in a drawer.

A USEFUL NEST OF TINY DRAWERS

There is nothing like having a proper place for everything.   With big articles it is easy enough to keep them where they may be found, but the small things, such as safety pins, hooks and eyes, snap fasteners, thimbles, etc., are easily lost unless a definite place is allotted to them. If you would like to make a useful little nest of drawers, just the thing for storing small odds and ends, here is the way.   Save up a dozen or more empty match boxes, and fix them all together by means of glue. Arrange them in four tiers of three, or three tiers of four, but two tiers of six would be an awkward shape.   Around the top, bottom and sides of the stack, paste a piece of artistic wallpaper, and see that it reaches to the extreme edges of the stack. Now slip the trays out of the boxes and paste strips of thin notepaper along their sides, then print neatly on the ends that show the names of the things which are to be kept in the respective boxes. If you would like to provide each drawer with a little handle, insert loosely a round-headed brass paper fastener.

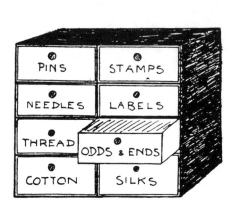

A Useful Nest of Tiny Drawers   For Soiled Hankies

FOR SOILED HANKIES

Take a piece of attractive silk, or failing that, some cretonne, about 16 inches long and 5 inches wide. Fold it in halves across the narrow width and cut away the corners in curves, so that you have a very long oval. Spread out the shape flat on the table and cut it down the centre for about a quarter of its length.

Next, fold the oval in halves, so that it is similar to what it was when you trimmed the corners, then take the head of a small doll. Xylonite ones can be bought for threepence. Place the head between the two curves of the oval and fold or bunch up the material around the neck. Then sew up the two sides, but first turn in the raw edges. You now have a kind of bag, with a doll's head peering out of the top.

You will remember that we cut a slit down the material. This should be arranged so that it comes to the front. Turn back the raw edges and sew them. Then, make a little bib, fix it round the doll's neck and let it hang down in front. Lastly, sew on a loop above the head.

When you have finished this attractive bag, hang it in your bedroom and stuff your soiled hankies in it. To do so you just lift up the bib, push them through the slit and let the bib drop again.

CROCHET

CROCHET HINTS

Different makes of wool vary considerable in thickness, so it is best to obtain the kind and quality advised when a book of instructions is being consulted, as, if a substitute is bought, you may find that the work, when completed, will not be of the size expected.

If you make a habit of working loosely, you will find that a smaller hook than the one recommended will help you to produce a tighter mesh ; on the other hand, if you usually work tightly, a larger hook than the one advised will enable you to produce looser work.

CROCHET CHAIN STITCH

This is the foundation of most crochet patterns. It may also be used as a trimming, in the form of braid, on some materials.

Hold the hook in the right hand and start by winding the wool once round the hook, making a loop ; pass the wool over the hook and draw it through the loop ; pass the wool again over the hook and draw it through the second loop, being careful to have only one stitch on the hook before making another stitch. Continue drawing the wool through each stitch left on the hook until you have made the length required.

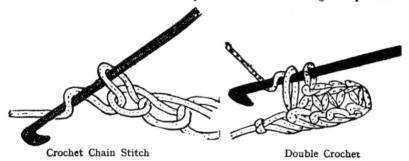

Crochet Chain Stitch   Double Crochet

DOUBLE CROCHET

First make a length of chain rather wider than the work is intended to be when finished. Hold the last chain stitch on the hook and pass the hook through the third chain from the end, pass the wool over the hook and draw it through the chain-stitch ; you now have two loops on the hook. Pass the wool over the hook again, and draw it through the two loops on the hook. Work the next stitch in the next chain in the same way.

TREBLE CROCHET

First make a long sequence of chains ; the trebles must be worked into this. Keep the last chain on the hook, pass the wool over and put the hook through the third chain from the hook. Pass the wool over the hook and draw it through the chain. You now have three loops of wool on the hook. Pass the wool over again and draw it through the first two loops, making a fresh loop ; pass the wool again over and draw it through the remaining two loops. You are now left with one loop, which you have just made. Do the next treble in the same way, working into the next chain and continue for the number of trebles required. See the illustration below.

LONG TREBLE CROCHET

Work this stitch in the same way as ordinary treble, but before passing the hook through the chain, wind the wool twice round the hook. Then draw a loop of wool through the chain, pass the wool over the hook and

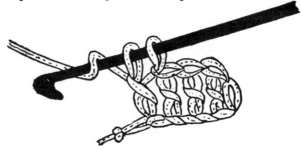

Treble Crochet

draw it through two loops ; pass the wool again over the hook and draw it through two more loops, and once more—wool over the hook and through the last two loops. Work the next long treble into the next chain in the same way.

SLIP STITCH OR SINGLE CROCHET

Pass the hook through a stitch, pass the wool round the hook and draw it through the stitch and through the loop on the hook at the same time.

Slip Stitch Crochet

This method is most frequently used when it is necessary to join together two pieces of crochet.

A DOLL'S CROCHET HAT

This little hat is easy to make and all you need in the way of material is some wool and a bone crochet hook. If you have not enough wool of one colour, but plenty of various shades, make a rainbow hat, working each row with a different colour.

Start by making 6 chain, and join it in a ring with one slip-stitch ;

make 2 chain, then into the ring work 12 double crochet, slip-stitch the last double crochet into the 2 chain of the same row ; make 2 chain, then, into the spaces between each double crochet of the previous row, work one double crochet, but into every fourth space make 2 stitches instead of 1, thus adding 4 stitches to the number in the row.   Do the next row in the same way and increase, as before, by working 2 double crochet into the space immediately above the one in which you increased in the previous row.

Continue increasing in each row until you have a circle of crochet large enough to cover the crown of the doll's head.   Now continue, row by row, making double crochet into each space, but without increasing, until a little cap is formed which fits over the head.

It will now be necessary to decrease in the next few rows until it is small enough to fit tightly to the head.   Before decreasing, count the number of stitches in the last row, divide this number by 4 and when you reach the space at each quarter of the way round, miss one space and work the double crochet into the next one.   In this way the row is decreased by 4 stitches.   Do the next row in the same way and decrease by missing 4 more spaces.   Continue like this until a tight band is formed which holds the cap on the head.   When completed, the hat is rather like a tam o'shanter.

INITIALS IN CROCHET

You may wish, at some time, to make use of initials on a piece of work. An excellent method, which serves the double purpose of embroidering, and supplying the letter at the same time, is to work a square of crochet, in the centre of which is the letter or letters required.

Start by making a length of chain, turn with 3 chain and work along the length required, making 1 treble, 2 chain, 1 treble, 2 chain, into the chain of the first row, and leaving 2 chain in this row, between each two single trebles.   This forms squares, known as *open mesh*, and is the most usual pattern for the ground work of simple designs in crochet. The initial is formed by working 2 trebles into each open mesh, instead of 2 chain between each two single trebles.   These solid squares of trebles must be arranged to mark the lines of the letters required.

You will be wise if you take a piece of squared paper—the kind used in children's arithmetic exercise books—and consider that each square represents one open mesh in crochet—that is, a square formed by 2 trebles with 2 chain between.   On this squared paper, first outline in pencil the initial desired.   Then darken each square through which the lines of the letter pass.   You may then imagine that the letter consists of solid squares of treble crochet, on a background of open meshes.   Elaborate the lines of the letter by adding extra squares at corners, or by making the vertical lines thicker by placing two squares side by side.   When you have evolved a satisfactory initial of the desired size, decide how large you wish the actual piece of crochet to be, and mark off an equal number of open squares at each side of the letter ; do the same at the top and bottom.

The alphabet on pp. 88-89 is suitable for crochet.   Use a fine steel hook—No. 5 is an easy size with which to work—and cotton which is not too fine, say No. 24.   Count the number of squares on the paper over which your design has been outlined, and for each square allow 3 chain. This will give you an idea as to the length of chain needed for the foundation. When you have worked the required length, turn with 3 chain, and make a few rows of open mesh, the exact number of these rows will depend on the size you wish the square to be. After you have worked

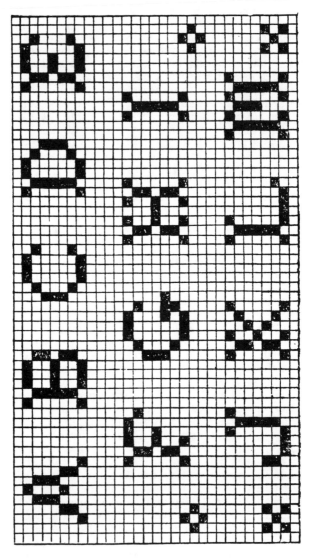

the right number it will be necessary to start the initial. Keep your pencilled design before you, and count the squares in it, as you proceed ; this will help you to place your letter in the centre of the square.

The piece of crochet filet, when completed, must be sewn to the material which it is intended to embroider, by means of a buttonhole stitch ; or, if preferred, the four sides of the square may be strengthened by working an edging of double crochet all round. This may then be oversewn to the article, and will prove a very strong and practical method of initialing.

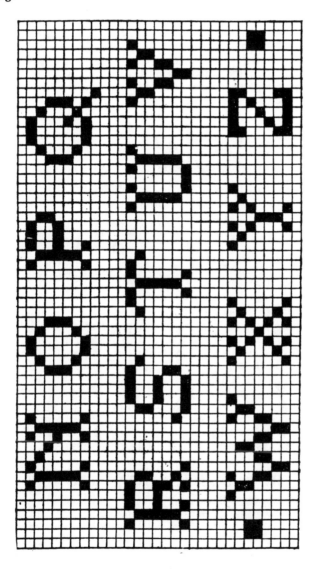

Afternoon tea-cloths, which have been trimmed with an edging of crochet, are much improved by the addition of an initial in one corner. This work is more simple to do than an elaborate design of fine embroidery or drawn-thread work, but is quite as effective in appearance.

M

HOW TO MAKE BEADS

There are several easy ways of making beads. Probably, the simplest plan is to make them of paper, with the aid of a knitting needle. First, obtain some long strips of paper, about half an inch wide, then coil about a yard of the paper around a knitting needle. Have a tube of glue handy, and when you have made about two complete turns of the paper, put a small dab of glue on it, to prevent it coming unwound. Then repeat the process when the end of the coil is reached.

The shape and size of each bead depends on the amount of paper used and the manner it is graduated. Long shapes are formed by lengthening out the coils along the needle, while round squat beads are the result of piling up the paper in a small space.

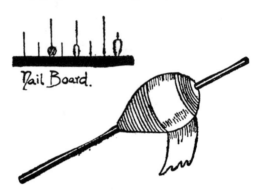

Nail Board.

When a bead has been formed, it is slipped off the needle, and, if it is to be coloured, it should be dropped into position on the painting board.

The latter is made by taking a long strip of wood or card, and driving a number of nails through it from the underside (see diagram). On the upstanding nails, the beads are stood, and it is easy to paint them without getting the hands in a mess.

We have, also, made beads by moulding little pellets of plastic wood around a needle. The material dries hard in a very little time, then the beads may be slipped off the needle and put on the nail board for painting. This method is quicker than the former, and, while the paper suits large beads, this way is more useful for those of medium size.

HOW TO MAKE BEAD FLOWERS

Bead work is a most fascinating pastime, which enables you to make all sorts of useful and decorative ornaments, suitable for wearing or displaying in the home. As a first lesson, we will suppose that you want to make a flower composed of a number of petals and a stalk.

How to make a Petal.—Take a long strand of thin flower wire, slip one bead on to it, and place it, approximately, half-way along the strand.

Next, slip two more beads on the strand, run them almost up to the first bead, bend the wire round so that the two beads come under the first bead, slip the free end of the wire through the two beads and pull both wires tightly. This provides the second row.

For the third row, slip three beads on the strand, on which you threaded the two beads, bend the wire round so that the three beads come under the two beads, slip the free end of the wire through the three beads and pull both wires tightly. This provides the third row.

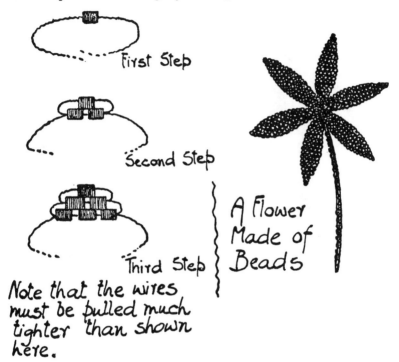

First Step

Second Step

Third Step

A Flower Made of Beads

Note that the wires must be pulled much tighter than shown here.

For the fourth, fifth, and many more rows, do exactly the same, but increase the beads each time by one.

As you will recognise, this lengthens the width of each row ; but, after a while, you will need to shorten each row, because a petal diminishes in width. To do this, you merely subtract a bead each time, just as you added one, in the commencement. When a petal has been formed, twist the two wires together, and turn to the second, third and other petals which you will shape in a similar manner. All the petals being made, the twisted wires of each are plaited together in one bunch, and the flower is finished.

How to make a leaf.—A leaf is made in exactly the same way as a petal, but it is, generally, considerably larger, and requires more rows and longer rows. The two ends of the wires are twisted together, finally, and they are plaited along with those of the petals.

A DANGLUMS FOR YOUR MOTOR CAR

Make this danglums for your car. Just fasten it above the look-out window at the back of your saloon car, and there it will swing and

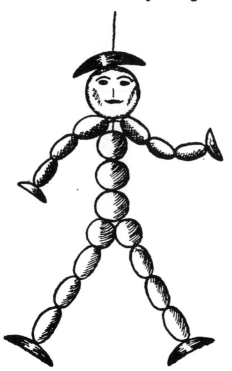

sway as long as the wheels turn round.

You will want some fairly large spherical and elliptical beads. Select wooden ones rather than glass or china, as, should the merry little fellow bounce against the window, he will not make such a clatter if he is wooden. You will, also, want a few buttons for feet, hands and hat.

By the way, do not thread the wire symmetrically through the holes in the hat button. Put it through one of the side holes, then his beret will be carried at a rakish angle. Do not use very thin wire, or Mr. Danglums will appear to be suffering from St. Vitus' dance.

A CHARMING BEAD NECKLACE

Would you like to make a charming bead necklace ? Here is the way :

Take two shades of beads, say red and gold ; though, of course, any two colours which match one of your frocks will do equally well.

Begin by using a long strand of cotton and a fine needle ; work with the cotton double, and put a large knot at the end.

These are the steps :

Thread one gold bead, three red, one gold, three red and four gold. Make a loop of these four gold beads by drawing the needle and cotton again through the first of these four, in the reverse direction, drawing the cotton quite tightly.

Add three red beads, one gold, and three red. Pass the needle and cotton again through the first gold bead of all. This completes one diamond.

Thread three red beads and one gold. These four form a straight edge at the top of the pattern (see A to B).

Now commence a second diamond, beginning from the point B. Thread three red beads ; then draw the needle and cotton through the gold bead at D. Add three more red beads, four gold and draw the needle through the first of these four, in the reverse direction, to form another gold loop.

Next, add three red beads, one gold and three red ; then draw the needle and thread through the gold bead shown at B. This completes the second diamond.

Follow by making the straight edge, B to C, and continue as described for the second diamond.

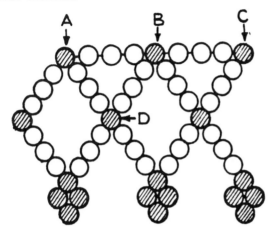

When you have made sufficient diamonds to go round your neck, fix a snap fastener (cost threepence) and the necklace is finished.

HOW TO MAKE A BEAD CURTAIN

First, decide on the rod which is to take the strands of beads. In making the selection, you must be guided by the conditions which exist. In some cases, a square rod serves best ; in others, a round one. Which-

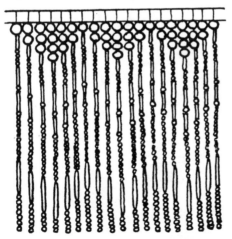

ever is decided upon, make a pencil mark along the entire length of the rod at every quarter or half inch. Then, make a slight cut with a pocket-knife or fine saw, where the pencil marks are.

Now, obtain some good macramé string and cut off a number of lengths. They should be as long as the curtain is desired, with two or three extra inches to spare.   Tie a piece of string at every cut in the rod, making the string sit into the cut.   In this manner, there is no opportunity for a strand to slide out of position.   Naturally, the string must be tied neatly and tightly around the rod and the free end should be carefully trimmed away.

To thread the beads, the rod is held downwards and the threading is done from above.   The pattern aimed at should be planned beforehand. As a rule, vertical lines do not look as well as those which rise and fall, as shown in the diagram.   For such lines, the lengths of string should have a graduated number of beads put on them, for the first and last bands of colour.   The intermediate bands will, of course, have the same number.   On the first strand, put, say, one bead ;   on the second, two beads ;   on the third, three beads ; . . . on the tenth, ten beads ;   on the thirteenth, nine beads, etc.

When each strand is fully threaded, make a knot, larger than the hole in the bead, and cut off the surplus string.

The rod can be painted in any desired colours, after the beads are threaded, if care is taken to see that the paint is not splashed.

ANOTHER WAY TO MAKE BEAD FLOWERS

All flowers do not consist of well-defined petals, and, accordingly, it is useful to know how to imitate those which resemble a tight rosette.

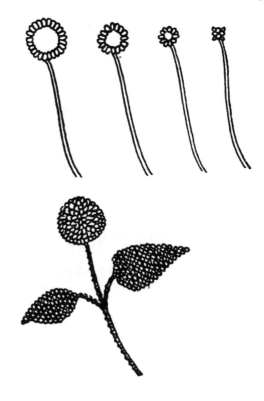

Take a number of beads, say forty small ones, and thread them on to a piece of wire. Form them into a ring, as shown in the first sketch.

Next, take thirty beads of the same size, thread and shape them as before. The second small sketch shows what is required.

Again take twenty beads of the same size and do as before (see third sketch).

Follow on with one or two even smaller rings.

Now, take the smallest ring and push the wire stalks through the centre of the second smallest ring. Having done this, push the four stalks through the next smallest ring and continue in the same way until all the rings are assembled together. You have a nicely domed rosette consisting of several rings, all of one colour, or of several, whichever you please.

The final steps are to plait all the wires, to make one stalk, and to add leaves, as already described.

TRIFLES IN BEADS AND BUTTONS

What a number of funny things to amuse children can be made out of beads and buttons strung on wire! We give just four things which we, ourselves, made in a quarter of an hour. You will admit that many youngsters would find them delightfully amusing. And, of course, you can sit down and make dozens of varied articles, just as quaint, in practically no time.

You will want a good assortment of beads, large and small, plump and slender, bright and sober in hue. As well, you will need an array of buttons. We hit upon a stall which was selling, for next to nothing, cards of buttons all different, which had been traveller's samples. They

had little value in the ordinary way because no two were alike; but it was just the thing for our work.

As to the beads, we think you will prefer the wooden ones to those of glass, because they are more strikingly coloured, and they will take better the pen work needed for making the faces, etc. This, by the way, is done with Indian ink.

To string the beads and buttons, you will need some wire. We, at first, used thin flower wire, but it allowed the legs and arms to tumble about, and we found fairly stout wire much better. It can be bent into positions which are more permanent.

There as just two points to remember. These things are for small kiddies to play with. So the ends of the wire must be carefully turned in with pliers and made smooth, to prevent scratching. Also, the little sections must be strung together strongly, so that there is no possible chance of any pieces coming loose. You know how youngsters put things in their mouths.

TOYS MADE OF COTTON REELS

Save all the used cotton reels that you can find and many will be the quaint toys that you can make with them. Try to get them of various shapes and sizes, so that when you have sawn them into pieces you will have an assortment of different parts.

Just to give you an idea of what can be done with them we print two illustrations. One shows five portions of different reels and the

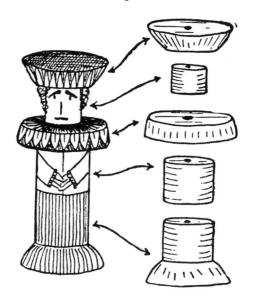

other the same portions when placed together and suitably ornamented. It represents an old lady who might be the queen in *Alice in Wonderland*.

To cut the reels, nothing is better than a fret-saw, though an ordinary tenon-saw will do almost as well, if used carefully. The parts are stuck together with tube glue, and the colouring is done with little tins of cellulose paint, which dries hard in a very short while. If the reels are clean they may be coloured with water-paints and lined with Indian ink ; but the effects will then be less vivid and attractive.

PLAIN SEWING

There are many stitches employed every day in plain needlework. An experienced worker soon learns which to employ under varying conditions, but the beginner may often be in doubt as to when it is necessary to use a " back-stitch " or a simple " running stitch," or when it is advisable to " whip " an edge or to turn in a hem. The following hints will be of assistance to the novice.

Running Stitch.—Pass the needle in and out of the material at regular distances, from the right side to the wrong, and up to the right side again. keep the stitches in a horizontal direction, from right to left of the work, and make three or four stitches on the needle at the same time, before drawing the thread through.

Back Stitching.—Make five or six running stitches, then insert the needle one stitch back from where the last stitch was finished ; make five or six more running stitches and one back stitch, and so on.

Hemming.—Trim the edge of the material perfectly straight by cutting along one thread. First, turn in the material, by folding the edge over to the wrong side to a depth of one eighth of an inch, along the whole length to be hemmed ; then again fold over the piece already turned in, not less than three sixteenths of an inch deep. The raw edge will then be protected by two thicknesses of the material. If a much wider hem is needed, the second fold may be made considerably deeper, but it must be kept in position by means of a tacking thread, that is, by making long running stitches through the three thicknesses of the material and making a back stitch at every fifth or sixth stitch. This prevents the tacking from puckering the work.

To stitch the hem, first tuck the end of the thread under the turned in edge of the fold ; then insert the needle under the fold and pass the point towards the left, taking up one or two threads directly under the fold and coming out through the two thicknesses at the edge of the fold. Make these stitches as small and regular as possible.

In turning up the bottom of a frock with a deep hem, the material is folded in the same manner as for ordinary hemming and the stitches are made in the same way ; that is, by taking up two threads of the material under the fold. But after each stitch the needle is passed between the two thicknesses which form the fold and is brought out at a place about half an inch to the left of the point where it was inserted. This method is quicker than ordinary hemming as the stitches are at least half an inch apart, which is a consideration when a long hem is to be worked. Also, on the right side of the work the stitches are so small and far apart that they are practically invisible.

Invisible Hemming.—It sometimes happens that a deep hem is out of place on the bottom of a frock ; or perhaps sufficient material may not have been allowed for the purpose. When this is so, the difficulty may be overcome by invisible hemming. This is a more modern and much neater method than plain hemming.

First turn the work inside out, then fold the raw edge over to the right side of the material to a depth of three-quarters of an inch. One

N

eighth of an inch below the fold, work small running stitches all round the width of the frock, working through the two thicknesses of the material and taking a back stitch occasionally, to prevent puckering.

Next open out the fold. The result will be that a small tuck is formed three-quarters of an inch from the raw edge on the wrong side of the material. Now turn in the raw edge twice towards the wrong side ; at the first fold, the edge is brought over until it rests along the top of the tuck ; it is then folded over again so that the tuck is enclosed and the edge of the first fold reaches the stitches which formed the tuck. These folds are kept in position by hemming them as neatly as possible, taking up at each stitch a tiny piece of material at the base of the tuck, and bringing the needle up through the several thicknesses at the edge of the fold. The stitches of the tuck should be completely hidden by the fold and the stitches of the hem should be invisible on the right side of the work. The hem, when finished, should have the appearance of a piping about one eighth of an inch deep, all round the bottom of the frock. The effect is much smarter than an ordinary hem and is suitable for the edge of a round collar or cuffs in addition to frock hems.

Hem Stitching and Picot Edging.—This is the first step in drawn thread work. It is used for so many purposes, and may be adapted to such a number of materials, that it is well worth learning to do it well. It is possible to put a picot edge to your own party frock frills, if you can hem-stitch neatly.

To start with, a few threads must be drawn right out of the material before the actual hemming can be done. First, loosen one end of a thread by means of a needle point. When the end of this thread has been picked out so that it is long enough to be held by the fingers, take it firmly with the right thumb and first finger, and pull at it steadily, but quietly, at the same time easing the material along this thread with the fingers of the left hand.

If the material is loosely woven, and if you are lucky, the whole length of thread will pull out without breaking. But it is more usual to be unlucky ; it is then necessary to lengthen again the end of this same thread, which has remained in the material, and then pull at it once more, repeating this until the whole piece of thread has been drawn out. You will find that, after one thread has been removed, no difficulty will be experienced in drawing out the others.

You may now begin the hemming. Use a small fine needle and fine cotton or silk, and start at the right hand of the work, stitching along the thread nearest to you. Insert the needle on the underside of the material, just below the upright threads, and draw it through to the right side. Now pass the needle under the first three or four vertical threads which have been left free after the horizontal threads have been drawn ; bring the needle from under these up to the right side again. You have picked up these threads with the one thread with which the needle is filled.

Now pass the needle again under these same three or four threads and put the point of the needle in the wrong side of the work, immediately below the last of the threads which are being picked up. Draw the needle through to the right side and pull the thread tightly. The first three or four threads are now drawn together at the lower edge.

Treat the next three or four in the same way, that is, pass the needle under them, draw it through on the right side, pass it under them again and draw it through the material just below the last thread, pull the needle tightly, and the second cluster of threads are hemmed together.

Proceed in this way until you have hemmed the entire length from which the threads have been drawn.

Now turn the work upside down and treat the opposite edge of the upright threads in the same way; but you must take care to pick up on the needle, each time, the same threads as were hemmed together along the other edge. In this way they will be gathered together in neat little bunches. A few threads of one bunch must not be mixed at one edge with a few threads of the next bunch. Each cluster must be quite apart from the other.

Plain hemming of straight edges is an uninteresting job, and is hardly suitable for such pieces of work as linen table-cloths, fancy table napkins, etc. For such things it is more usual to finish the sides with hem-stitch. Before drawing the threads, decide what width hem will be required; then from the edge mark off a distance just a little more than double this width, and at this point draw two or three threads parallel to the edge; do the same to every side of the work, being careful that the threads shall be drawn at an equal distance from every edge. Now turn in the raw edges narrowly along their whole length; turn this over again, making the first fold just touch the line from which the threads have been drawn, and tack it down all round to keep it in place.

It is now ready to be hemmed. Do this in the same way as described above, but take care to pass the needle through the several thicknesses of material where it is turned in. When you have stitched along this side, the tacking threads may be removed. Work round each edge in the same way and hem along the opposite line of the upright threads as before.

This is a much more effective method of finishing off a hem than plain hemming. Linen collars and cuffs look very smart if worked with a hem of this kind, especially if a fine brightly coloured thread or silk is used for the stitching.

To produce a picot edge as a trimming is not a difficult matter. You must first draw a few threads and hem along both sides as described above. Then take a pair of small sharp scissors and carefully cut along the centre of the upright threads, thus dividing the material into two pieces, each with one side which is picot edged. This method is particularly suitable for frills; it is much smarter than machine-stitching along the lower edge, and if the hemming is done in a shade of silk to contrast with the material, a touch of colour is introduced which will look so attractive that no other kind of trimming will be needed for the dress.

Felling.—There are several ways of stitching and finishing seams. To make a *Flat Seam*, lay the two edges which are to be joined exactly together, one above the other, with the right sides of the material facing, and tack them together. Then stitch along the line of tacking thread with a neat running stitch, taking one back stitch occasionally. When the whole length has been stitched together, trim away half the under edge very carefully; fold the upper edge over the lower one and turn it in (as for hemming) and hem it neatly down to the material beneath. This is called *felling*. When finished, the seam should lie quite flat.

Over-Sewing a Seam.—When it is necessary to join two selvedges together, they may be over-sewn. First tack them, to keep the edges in position.

Insert the needle straight through from the back selvedge to the nearer one, picking up one thread of each edge. Make the next stitch two threads to the left of the first one. Do not draw the working thread too tightly, or it will not lie flat on the right side. Press along the over-sewn stitches with the thimble, when the seam is finished. This will flatten it.

A French Seam.—This method is most frequently used for the under-arm seams of sleeves ; or when working on a very flimsy material, such as georgette, which is liable to fray.

Begin by running the two edges together as for a flat seam, but place the *wrong* sides of the material together and work the running stitches along the right side of the material. Then turn the work over, so that the right sides face each other, press along the seam with the fingers, in order to flatten it, and work a running stitch along the seam again, taking care that the two raw edges are enclosed between the second row of stitches and the first seam. When the work is turned right side up, no frayed threads should emerge through the stitches of the second row of running.

Gathering.—Superfluous fulness is gathered by making one row of running stitches, parallel to the edge of the material to be gathered, and across the material from one selvedge to the other. Work several stitches at once on the needle before drawing it out each time ; this enables the work to be done quickly, the stitches are more equal in size, and the gathers are formed at the same time.

Stroking Gathers.—A thread having been run through the material which is to be gathered, it must now be drawn up so that all the fulness is bunched together ; do not break off the thread, but wind it round a pin, which is pushed in at the point where the gathers end. Hold the work firmly in the left hand, and with the right, take a strong needle and draw its point down the material between the gathers, thus regulating them ; begin at the left edge of the gathers and work towards the right, and as you proceed, hold the fulness in place with the left thumb. Then turn the work the other way up, and in the same way stroke along the gathers on the other side of the gathering thread.

Button Holes.—First mark the length of the hole which is needed to fit the button, by means of two rows of running stitches, worked two or three threads apart, over the spot where the button hole is to be. Between these two rows of stitches make a perfectly straight slit. This must lie horizontally across the material, not vertically, unless you have some special purpose in view, such as a very large button.

Put the needle in at the back of the work and bring it through at the lower left hand corner of the slit, just below the line of running stitches.

Then put the needle in again at the back of the work, about two threads to the right of the first stitch, picking up three threads on the lower edge of the slit ; at the same time, wind the thread with which you are working round the point of the needle, from the right to the left, and draw out the needle through the loop, thus making a tight loop or knot on the edge of the slit. Work along the lower edge, continue round the curve at the end, and turn the material so that every stitch is made towards you. Place each stitch as near to the previous one as possible, until you reach the spot where you began.

To finish the button-hole securely and prevent it from fraying when the button is pushed through, it is advisable to make a bar across the end of the hole at the point which the stitching began and ended. Do not break off the thread when the hole has been stitched round ; instead, sew two or three stitches across the end of the hole, and work buttonhole stitch over them, thus making a strong bar which prevents the hole from stretching or splitting.

A LONG-CLOTHES BABY DOLL

This doll is quite easy to make, especially if you happen to have a baby doll's head and face of which use can be made. If no suitable head is available, then you must make one.

Decide first on the size of doll desired and cut out a paper pattern approximating the shape of the front half of the baby's face, i.e., make a circle of paper, then shape off slightly one-half of the circumference for the forehead, leaving the other half quite circular, to act as a chin with fat cheeks. With this paper as a pattern cut out two pieces of butter muslin and two pieces of pale pink material, preferably velvet. Place these rounds together in the following order :

(1) A velvet circle, wrong side up.
(2) A muslin circle to face the right side of the velvet circle.
(3) A muslin circle to face the first muslin circle.
(4) A velvet circle right side to face the muslin circle.

Pick up these four circles in the order suggested and machine them together round the edges, leaving about one and a half inches unstitched at the top of the head. Turn these inside out by means of the unstitched portion, thus placing the muslin circles outside and the velvet inside. Have a supply of soft rags, cut small in readiness, and stuff these through the opening in the head, till a firm cushion is produced ; then stitch up the opening securely.

The next thing is to make the body, arms, and legs. As before, cut a paper pattern first, nearly square and on the large size. Place this square flat on a table and lay the head at one side of it. You can then get some idea of the size the body ought to be, and this square can easily be reduced in size by cutting the edges till it appears just a little larger than seems in correct proportion to the head.

Using this as a pattern, cut out as before two pieces of muslin and two of velvet. Machine these four together in the same way as was done for the head, leaving a one-inch gap in the stitching. Turn this inside out and stuff with small rags and paper shavings. In just the same way make four small oblong cushions to represent the arms and legs, and when these are stuffed, stitch them to the body, two on one side for legs and the other two at opposite corners for arms. Sew the head to the side of the body above the corners to which the arms were attached, being careful to place the wider part of the head on the body. Take some black wool and, by means of big stitches on the forehead, a fringe is supplied. Two horizontal stitches beneath the fringe serve as eyebrows. Red wool acts as nose-tip and lips; and bright blue wool gives the eyes. Dab some red water-paint on each cheek. Finish off the head by means of a little lace-edged muslin bonnet, which hides the stitches round the head and comes down a little way over the fringe.

A simple long-clothes nightie may be made easily, with little sleeves, and sewn to the body at the neck. Tie some coloured ribbon round the waist and some more at each wrist and at the neck. Allow a small part of each rag arm to emerge from the sleeves, and on each of these extremities work some black stitches to give the effect of fingers.

The baby is now made!

A TEA-COSY FOUNDATION

First decide on the size and shape of the cosy. The ordinary domed variety is easy to make, and there are so many ways of ornamenting it, that perhaps it will be advisable to make your first attempt of this shape.

A moderate size will be 12 inches across and 10 or 11 inches high. Cut out four pieces of material, all of the same size and of the same

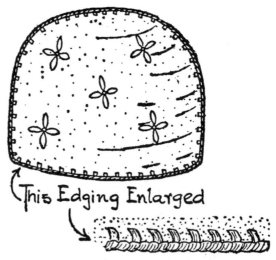

This Edging Enlarged

material, or two of one colour and two of another. Take two, intended for the inside of the cosy, and machine or run them together all round the curved sides. Do the same with the two pieces intended for the outside and then turn it right side out.

Use wadding as an inter-lining for padding purposes; cut two pieces of the same shape and size as the four pieces of the material, tack round the curved sides of these in the same way as you did for the covering.

Now put the three shapes together ; first take the inside shape and turn it so that the right side is inside ; slip this inside the wadding shape and tack the two together all round the curved sides, slip over them the outside cover, placing the right side outside. Turn in the straight sides, and stitch neatly round the lower edge of the cosy, taking care to tuck in any pieces of wadding that may peep out.

If bright coloured velveteens or silks are used, very little in the way of trimming will be required. Perhaps a ruching, if the material is silk, will give the necessary finishing touch ; while a plain-coloured cord is all that will be needed to trim the edges, if the cosy is of velvet or velveteen.

If, however, the outside of the cosy is made of plain linen, or a similar material, it could be ornamented with an embroidered design in the centre of each side, using a washing embroidery thread of bright hue for the purpose. The sides could be edged with a chain stitch of the same bright thread, as described on page 30.

A FRILLED LAMPSHADE

Pretty shades for the electric light make such a difference to the appearance of a bedroom ! If your light is a single electric bulb, hanging from the ceiling, you can easily make a shade which will be really pretty. There is probably a globe of some kind round your bulb ; if so, you will not need a wire frame as foundation ; this globe will do instead. First measure the height of it, from the part which hangs from the wire to its lowest point ; the material for your shade must be two inches deeper than this measurement. Next measure the width all round the widest part of the glass shade, either at the bottom edge, or round the middle, whichever bulges most. The material of the new shade must be two or three inches wider than this.

Choose silk, muslin, flowered voile, or even cretonne, if it is not too stiff, for the substance of the shade. Cut one strip of the selected material two inches deeper and three inches wider than the measurements which you have taken. Join the two sides by running them together, on the wrong side ; then turn in the raw edges once, and hem them down neatly on the wrong side. Now turn in the edge intended for the lower hem of the shade, and run it neatly on the wrong side. From the piece of material from which you have cut the shade, now cut some straight strips, from one and a half to two inches deep—these are to act as frills. If you have been able to arrange for the selvedge to form one side of these strips, you will save a good deal of work, as then there will be no need to hem the edge of the frills. But if there is no selvedge, one side of the strips must be turned in as narrowly as possible, and hemmed or machined down. Each frill must be one and a half times as wide as the width of the shade.

Turn in the top edge, after the lower has been hemmed, run a tacking thread through it and draw the frill up loosely by means of this thread. Now stitch this frill on the shade, placing the gathers about one inch above the hem, and arrange them evenly, as you sew on the frill. Fix a second frill in the same way, and sew it about one inch higher than the first one ; if you desire a third, sew it in the same way, one inch above the second.

When all the frills have been attached satisfactorily, turn in the top edge of the shade, about one and a half inches all round and hem it neatly.   Midway between this stitching and the top of the shade, run another row of stitches, making a slot into which some narrow tape must be threaded, by means of a bodkin.   This produces a small up-standing frill at the top of the shade ; keep the ends of the tape free. The shade is now finished, and ready to be put over the light.

Slip it over the glass shade and draw up the tape so that the top edge is gathered tightly and firmly.   Secure the ends of the tape and tuck them in so that they cannot be seen.   Now pull the frills down carefully in order to conceal the electric bulb as much as possible ; the lowest frill ought to hang a little below the tip of the bulb.

If bright colours have been used, this shade ought to look very attractive.

Stiff material, such as muslin, should be used if there is no glass shade underneath, acting as a foundation.   You will find that the stiffness of this kind of material will be sufficient to give shape to it, without the need of a support.

LOOSE COVERS FOR EASY CHAIRS

Loose covers are generally made of cretonne, printed linen or chintz, all of which will wash well or submit to a dry cleaning process.   These materials are usually sold in two widths—single width, which is 31 inches wide, and double width, which is 50 inches and upwards.   The former suffices for the average armchair.

In selecting a pattern, do not forget that some are much more difficult to work with than others. The easiest of all is a small, all-over, non-descript pattern, which looks much the same whether placed upright, sideways, tilted or inverted. There is no worry then in getting the lines straight or the design central. Moreover, there is far less waste in matching the material. If a striped material is fancied, choose one that has the lines recurring at no great distance. Should there be three or four different stripes and each fairly wide, the waste is considerable.

To estimate the amount of material required is generally the first consideration. If 31 inch stuff is bought, a fairly accurate idea of the quantity can be gained by taking the following measurements and adding them together:

(1) Inside back, from top to bottom, with extras for tucking in at the seat and for reaching a few inches over the head.

(2) Length of seat from front to back with a few inches extra for tucking in at back. Multiply this by three if a loose cushioned seat is being considered.

(3) Length of back (outside) from top to bottom of the chair.

(4) Twice the length from arm (from cushion inside) to lowest part of the chair (outside).

(5) Length of panel on front of arm. Two panels can be cut side by side, or in one operation by folding the material vertically.

(6) Length of cheek or ear, if present. The width of material will permit of the pieces being cut out side by side.

(7) Add sufficient for valance, if required.

(8) Depth of front panel, from seat to bottom edge.

(9) Add sufficient for any places where it is necessary to extend the width of material.

o

As a guide, it may be added that an average easy chair takes eight or nine yards of 31 inch material.

Cutting the material to shape is a matter which troubles the beginner. In such cases it is advisable to make a set of paper patterns for the purpose. The expert does not trouble about such details, however. He folds the material double and places it on half the chair. Then he indicates where the cutting is to be done by means of a piece of tailor's chalk. It is highly important to remember to allow for turnings.

Of course, it is not always possible to make the cover fit the chair exactly, because rolls and curves cannot be followed on occasions. All that can be hoped for is as near a fit as is practical, always remembering that a loose cover should not be too loose.

Covers that are for ever getting out of position are a nuisance. To keep the seat from pulling out, fit an extra flap of material, at the back of the cover, which may be tucked in the gap at the back of the seat where it joins the chair back. A cushion, made to fit the seat, will also help considerably in holding the material in place. Also sew on tapes to tie round the legs. These will keep the cover shipshape more than anything else.

DAINTY GARTERS

Pretty garters are much cheaper to make at home than to buy; so save all your odd bits of ribbon and coloured silks; they may come in useful in an emergency when a present is needed in haste.

Elastic of the usual garter width is required, sufficient to make two garters, also 1½ inch wide ribbon, twice as long as the elastic; and plain tape of the same length as the ribbon, but ½ inch narrower.

Divide the ribbon and tape into two equal lengths. Place one piece of tape on to a piece of ribbon so that the centres of each are together, and, with the machine, stitch each edge of the tape to the ribbon, leaving a ¼ inch border of ribbon beyond each tape edge. Treat the second piece of ribbon and tape in the same way. Take the two lengths of elastic and thread each into the slots formed by the tape on the ribbon. Stitch the ends of the elastic securely to one another and arrange the extra length of ribbon and tape along the elastic ring thus formed, so that the ¼ inch edge of ribbon makes a tiny frill at each edge of the garter. Make two neat little bows or rosettes, and fasten them to the join of the ribbon, thus hiding the stitches. Artificial flowers, placed in a tiny tight bunch, also act as a pretty ornament on dainty garters. Or small artificial flowers might be placed at regular intervals round the ribbon garter to form a flowery wreath.

A USEFUL APRON

An apron, made all by yourself, which you can wear when doing odd jobs, is something of which to be proud.

First, obtain a pretty piece of cretonne or a plain strip of suitably coloured casement cloth. Measure yourself from the knees, upwards, over the shoulders and to the back of the arms. This will give the length of the strip needed. The width is that of your chest measurement, from under one arm to the other.

Place the material flat upon the work-table and cut out the oval, as shown in the diagram ; then trim away the upper corners. The bottom of the oval should come roughly, a third of the way down the material.

Slip the oval over your head and decide where the waist line is to be. Make a mark there, so that you will know where to sew on the apron strings.

From another piece of material, make a wide pocket, almost equal to the width of the apron and any depth that is useful ; turn in the raw edges and sew along three sides to the first strip of material. Arrange for the top line to come at the waist level.

Hem all the edges of the apron, not already sewn, and then make two apron strings. Cut these out of scraps of the material, 3 inches wide, folded to make a width of about one inch, and sew in position.

Your apron is finished.

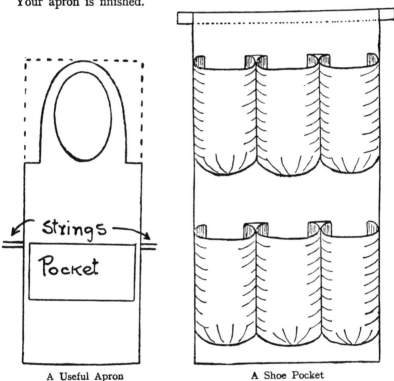

A Useful Apron   A Shoe Pocket

A SHOE POCKET

You know how untidy shoes look when they are left to lie on the floor of your bedroom. Not only do they spoil the appearance of the room, but the shoes, themselves, are very easily damaged, if they are not kept in some suitable place.

Here is a capital idea which will help in making your room tidy, and, at the same time, it will guard your foot-wear against unnecessary damage. The idea is to make a hanging shoe pocket.

In the diagram, we show exactly what the shoe pocket looks like.

Our picture gives a pocket for three pairs, but, of course, you can make your pocket for any number of pairs.

For a three-pair pocket, a piece of gay coloured cretonne, about a yard long and 18 inches wide, is needed. This will allow for turnings and the making of a wide hem, at the top, for taking a round curtain rod, which fixes, at the ends, into a pair of brass curtain supports. You can place these on the inside of your wardrobe door, on the bedroom door, or anywhere preferred.

The diagram shows that the contrivance is made up of a back-cloth and two long strips of similar material, which constitute the pockets. The strips should be about 28 inches long and 10 inches wide. These dimensions vary, however, according to the size of the shoes and the height of the heel. For this reason, it is advisable to plan the pockets with a sample shoe before you.

The upper edge of the strip is put on horizontally, and it had better be sewn, in position, first. After that, the sides of each pocket are stitched three quarters of the way down. Then the bottom part is bunched together in pleats.

Naturally, a shoe fits into its pocket with the toe downwards.

A KEY RACK

Keys are tiresome things to carry about and they are still more of a nuisance when they become mislaid. To overcome these troubles, make a key rack and hang it in a convenient spot, where all at home may have ready access to it.

The rack is very easily made. Take a piece of wood 12 inches long and about 6 inches wide. Obtain a nice piece of cretonne or furnishing silk, stretch it over the wood and, having folded in the corners neatly, tack it down on the underside. Then, screw in a row of small cup-hooks, on the face side and a pair of brass ears, on the opposite side. These ears will support the board on two nails. Accordingly, they must be equi-distant from the upright sides of the board.

If you care to embellish the rack, cut out a key-shaped piece of dark material and stitch it horizontally above the row of cup-hooks.

A BAG FOR CLOTHES-LINE PEGS

Anything that saves time and labour in the household duties is worth considering. The following bag offers a number of points in this direction. First, it saves a great deal of stooping, when hanging out the clothes on washing day ; then, it keep the pegs in a place where they can always be found ; and, not the least feature about it, it is ornamental.

Purchase half a yard of towelling and procure an ordinary penny coat-hanger. Fold over an inch of the material, along the short end, make a hole in the centre, slip the hook of the hanger through the hole and sew up the fold, so that the hanger is held tightly. If the hanger happens to be longer than the width of the towelling, cut a small piece off each end.

Next, fold the towelling in halves, lengthwise, and sew up the two sides. You now have a neat bag in which to keep the clothes-pegs.

When hanging out the washing, the bag is just hooked on to the line, in some convenient position and there is no need to keep continually bending down, when a peg is wanted.

Naturally, you may wish to ornament the bag. This is easily done in several ways. You can embroider the shape of some pegs on both sides of the bag, you can sew on some large discs of coloured casement cloth, or follow any plan which you fancy.

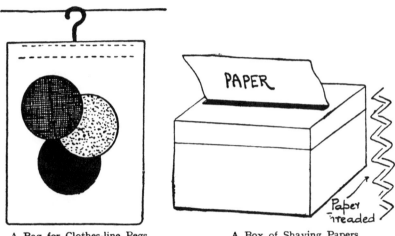

A Bag for Clothes-line Pegs   A Box of Shaving Papers

A BOX OF SHAVING PAPERS

Any man who still shaves with an ordinary razor will welcome one of these boxes of shaving papers, because they have the merit of being tidy and easy to handle. They are certainly an improvement on the pads which most men use.

First, obtain some thin typewriting paper of the kind that is sold for duplicating. You can get it in a pleasant shade of blue, pink, orange, green, etc., for a shilling a ream, quarto size. Take twenty sheets and cut each into four. You will now have eighty pieces. Trim a small strip off each and then fold the sheets across the middle. The pack will now fit comfortably in a cardboard " fifty " cigarette box of the Gold-flake type.

Now, this is the only tedious part. Feed the sheets one into the other zig-zag fashion, as shown in the small illustration. Get them all to fold over nicely or they may catch when being used. Having threaded all the eighty pieces, slip an elastic band round them so that they will not fly up and get out of order.

Turn to the box. Cut a line long-ways through the lid, from end to end. This line must be a little longer than the length of the papers, and it should be about an eighth of an inch wide. It will be quite easy to cut if the lid is placed flat on a sheet of glass, inside upwards, and the cutting is done with a sharp pocket knife.

The next thing is to cover the whole of the outside of the box with a smart piece of wallpaper.

You now return to the stack of papers, and removing the elastic band, put them inside the box. The top paper is half threaded through the slit in the lid, the box is closed and two or three papers are withdrawn to see if they feed through properly. When you are satisfied that they do, a narrow band of the same wallpaper is pasted round the lid to close the box effectively. It is now ready for use.

When the box is empty, the band is torn off. A new stack of papers is prepared and put inside, and a fresh strip of paper is pasted on to replace the old one.

A MOTTO BOARD

What is your favourite motto? Whether you fancy one or not it is quite certain that it is a wise thing to have one displayed where you can see it constantly. A very easy and attractive way of keeping a motto before your notice is to print the words on a little board and to hang it in your bedroom.

This is one attractive method, which you might care to follow : Procure a piece of three-ply wood and cut out a section, 12 by 8 inches. Do not trust to the eye for getting the lines straight, and the corners, right angles. Use a ruler and a straight edge or set-square. When the board is cut out, rub the face and the edges with fine glass-paper to make them smooth and clean.

Then rule a pencil line all round the edges, but a quarter of an inch from them, then write or print the wording you have chosen, in a neat fashion. Be careful of the spacing and be sure that it is spaced suitably for the purpose.

Then get two steel knitting needles, place the tip of one in the fire, and, when it is red hot, grip it by means of a duster or a kettle-holder, and trace the pencil lines with it. While you are using the first needle, put the second one in the fire to heat, so that you can continue with it when the first one has cooled down. Use them alternately, in this way, until all the tracing is finished.

The hot needles will burn their way slightly into the board and cause brown marks, which show up very well on a light coloured wood.

A LEATHER CASE FOR MATCH BOOKS

Match books are preferred to boxes of matches, by many people, because they are less bulky to carry, and they do not bulge out the pockets or hand bags. But a match book, if appearances are considered, should be carried in a neat leather case.

To make a suitable case, choose a strip of leather that is nice and supple, and which will not add any appreciable bulk to the book itself. A piece of velvet Persian, of an attractive shade, may go very well, but more than likely it will be a trifle too limp, and, probably, a thin calf-finished Persian will answer better.

Just how long and how wide the strip must be depends on the size of the match book, but five by one and three-quarter inches will be approximately correct. The exact measurements can be determined by wrapping the leather round a case of matches. Remember that it must overlap where the press button comes—i.e., about three-quarters of an inch.

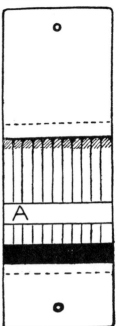

Do the cutting on something flat, and use a knife. At the same time, shape up another strip of leather, half an inch wide and as long as the width of the large piece of leather. This is fitted, later on, as a band under which the flap of the match book is slipped and held firmly. One thing more—trim the four corners of the large strip, so that they are neatly curved.

The next step is to procure a book of matches and to fold the leather round it. If the material refuses to fold snugly round the case, and prefers to bulge, just give it a wipe over the entire surface with a wet rag and press the folds with a warm iron. Of course, the leather must not be folded round the matches when the iron is used.

Now, we come to the decorative part. There are several ways of making the case appear very attractive, but what we suggest is the following: Prick holes around the entire edge of the strip of leather with an awl, making them an eighth of an inch apart. Be very careful that they are all in line Then, sew through the holes with a silk thread of a colour that pleases you. Use the thread double and make the stitches lap round the edge of the case. Pull the thread just tight enough to fit round without any slack, and, equally important, do not have it so tight that the leather is puckered.

Next, place the narrow cross band in the position shown at A, and sew through the two thicknesses.

The last operation is to fit the press-button. If you lack the proper supplies for doing this work, you can find an old glove, take the fastener from it and use the two halves. The blade of a pocket-knife will open out the pressed edges and help to fix them in their new home. Another plan is to dispense with a fastener altogether, to cut the flap of the leather into the shape of a tongue, and arrange for it to slip into a slot in the under fold of the material.

HOW TO CUT A STENCIL PLATE

Stencil plates in a variety of designs may be bought for a few pence, but most girls will far prefer to make their own, not on the score of expense so much as because home-made stencils can be shaped to fit exactly the work in hand.

If you wish to cut your own plates, either procure some oiled or waxed papers, such as are used by typists for duplicating purposes, or get a few sheets of tough cartridge paper, and, when the cutting is finished, coat both sides with shellac varnish.

The selection of the design requires some care. Only those will serve which can be made to look effective when each portion of the picture may be isolated from the next portion. The whole appearance thus depends upon masses placed near together. Rings and circles, for instance, are, of course, impossible, as the centres would drop out ; but if a little bridge of paper, known as a tie, can be left here and there to hold the centres in place, the trouble is obviated.

Having made the design, transfer it to the waxed paper and begin the cutting.   Place the sheet on a piece of glass and cut along the lines of the design with the tip of a sharp pocket-knife.   As the knife travels, it should be preceded by the thumb of the left hand, and followed by the index finger of the same hand.   This will prevent the paper riding off the sheet of glass and so becoming torn.   Cut the corners of the design with especial care, and, in order that they shall be neatly made, draw the knife away from angles and not towards them.

In the case of involved designs, begin cutting in the centre and work to the outer parts.   This direction minimises tearing.   Never help a mass to fall out ; it should fall out of its own accord as soon as the complete cut has been made.

HOW TO STENCIL A DESIGN

Hundreds of things in the home can be made beautiful by means of the stencilling art.   For the work, you will need an assortment of paper stencil plates, some suitable paints, a bottle of stencilling medium,

and one or more stencil brushes.   Oil colours are necessary when stencilling on wood, metal, glass, leather, and walls generally, but water colours serve for most fabrics and paper, as long as " fixed " paints are used. Mix oil with turpentine or " medium," and water colours with water. The necessary brushes are of the stumpy, flat-headed bristle kind, something like a small shaving-brush, with the tip ground flat. Have one brush for each main colour if you can afford them.

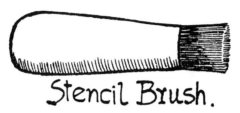

Stencil Brush.

To do the actual stencilling, mix the paints fairly thickly. Apply them by holding the brush perfectly upright, and then dab. Do not resort to a painting action, as this will cause the colour to creep under the stencil and obliterate part of the design. To keep the stencil still, pin it to the material, and if the fabric is of delicate texture, place a piece of blotting paper underneath it. Wipe the stencil plate on both sides each time it is lifted off the material.

A Few Precautions.—Try your hand on an old piece of material before attempting to decorate a useful article. Use as little colour as will do the work. Always dab the brush on a piece of fabric before applying it to the actual work. When patterns are to be repeated use a guide line to ensure continuous straight lines.

HOW TO MAKE A WIRE NAME BROOCH

Wire brooches are very fascinating and when one becomes fairly facile with the small pliers used, they are not very difficult to make.

It is best to use gold-filled wire, and it is not very expensive. The brooch-pin is made first ; there is no need to cut your wire to any particular length, as the unworked part will serve as a handle while the design is in progress. Estimate the length the whole brooch is likely to be, and allow an extra half inch in case of error. Bend the pin as in Fig. A, remembering that the pin is to be kept to the back and that it governs the central line of the brooch. Fig. B explains itself and illustrates the general principle of working. Always remember that the lines forming the design must be kept to the front, while the construction lines carrying the wire, from point to point of the design proper, are turned behind, towards the pin. Work carefully and you will not find it too difficult a task.

We will take a rather elaborate name, such as ELIZABETH. Here it will be well to write out the name first and think out every turn before commencing with the wire. The illustration C will make it clear that it is impossible to dot the letter " i," and you will note that an abrupt turn of line must be avoided if possible. Holding the wire by the long piece, or coil, give the pin a bend backwards to make it stand far enough away from the brooch proper. Then coil it upward to the top of the letter E, making a long loop ; a smaller curl (to the front) for the middle

P

of the E ; and a large circle (finishing behind) for the foot of the capital letter.

The tops of the letters I and T, the centre downstroke of Z, and the foot of H, are the only places where an abrupt turn is made and these cannot be avoided.

The construction of the hook for the brooch pin follows on the last letter (Fig. D). A curl round the shaft of the hook itself, and your wire

takes a graceful curve above and behind the name towards the foot of the initial letter E. A couple of sharp twists round the bend of the pin are given and then the wire may be nipped off.

To finish the brooch, cut off the extra half inch left in doubt, if it has not been used up, and with a smooth file bring the pin to a sharp point.

A GARDEN HAMMOCK

If you have some strong trees in your garden, you will value a hammock for the hot, sunny days that we dream about but only rarely get. You will find that a network hammock takes rather a long time to make, and we, personally, find it a difficult thing into which to climb. Much better, in our estimation, is the kind made of striped canvas, of the sort used for deck chairs and sun blinds. You will want between three and four yards of material, and let it be fairly wide, say a yard and a half.

Now, take two pieces of wood an inch in section, and a little longer than the width of the canvas. Before doing anything else, see that the two cut edges of the material are at right angles with the selvedge sides. You can do this quite accurately enough with a T-square and a long lath. If they are not at right angles, make them so, because, if they are not true, the hammock might always dip to one side.

The next thing is to place one of the wooden lengths flush with the edge of the canvas, allowing the wood to project at both ends equally. Now drive in three or four nails. You will not want long, small-headed nails that will go right through the wood and out the other side. Get what are called clout nails. They are short and stumpy, but strong, and they have big heads. Now, roll the wood over once only. Put in three or four more nails. Roll it over once again and drive in still more nails. Again, roll the wood over a *complete turn* (four times) and put in a good number of nails. Then that end is finished. Do exactly the same at the other end.

The final operation is to take some rope and hang the hammock between two trees. Here, we cannot give you exact measurements, because everything depends on the distance apart of your two trees, and the position of the branches round which you intend to loop the rope. But this much can be said. Use sash cord, not any piece of old rope that may look strong, but will be weak in certain parts. Have double supports at each end, so that if one lot goes wrong, the other will still do its work. Let one be looped round the projecting ends of the stick and the other pierced through the wood and tied.

Lastly, clear the space under the hammock. Do not have flower-pots, glass jars, upstanding sticks, or wire work on the ground below.

IF YOU CAN PRINT

If you can print, here is a way of amusing your friends. Our sketch shows some very long attenuated printing which can only be read with difficulty. In fact, you will have to hold it up to the level of your eye

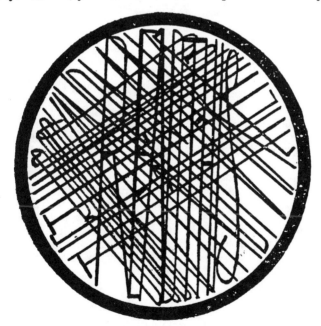

and look at it while it is almost horizontal if you want to find out w hat it says. Do some printing in this way and see if your friends can r ead it. Just note that the narrower each letter is, the harder it will be to recognise.

HOW TO DECORATE YOUR HAMMOCK

The illustration of the hammock will give you the best idea for decorating, and I think you will agree that it is much nicer for the trimmings. With a little time spent on it, this popular garden " couch " can be made very artistic, and there are a hundred and one ways of ornamentation.

There is not room here to go into any one method in detail, but the illustration, together with these notes, will be sufficient to give you the idea. A little ingenuity brought to bear will suggest additions and alterations to suit all. The accompanying sketch gives the idea for

hanging lapels ; these can be made of almost any material to hand, though stained canvas is suggested as being the most suitable, and this can be hand-painted or embroidered in any design or colour to suit the fancy.

To add such a decoration to the hammock gives it a more solid appearance, like a couch, in addition to making it more artistic. Put each lapel on separately ; this will prevent them from buckling when the hammock is in use. A very nice blend of colours is to have flax or natural coloured canvas (which, by the way, does not show the dust), with the design in purple and orange. In most hammocks we find one or more pillows or cushions—it would be nice to have these decorated in the same manner as the hammock.

A HEARTH BROOM

This little broom, which we are about to describe, is a really useful article, as well as one that is quaint and decorative. In addition, it makes a nice present, since everybody has a hearth that needs tidying up several times a day, in the winter months.

First obtain three pieces of rope, each about 2 feet long. Put them

side by side and tie them together in a bunch about 7 inches from one
end. Then, plait the
three long pieces and, as
this part is to serve as
the broom handle, you
may think it advisable to
wind them around a pea-
stick. This will give the
handle a certain amount
of rigidity. When you
come to the end of the
rope, tie a piece of string
round the pieces to pre-
vent them untwisting.

The next step deals
with the short, unplaited
end. Unravel each piece
of rope, from the tip up
to the string binding and,
then, comb all the
strands, so that they
make one good sized
mop. It may be advisable to trim this mop with scissors to make it an
even round shape.

When this is done, obtain some strands of raffia and twist them
spirally round the handle. Bind the two ends with short pieces of raffia
and, if you like, tie a loop and a tassel to the top end.

We have made several hearth brooms on these lines. In some cases,
we have omitted to plait the lengths of rope, merely placing them evenly
round the pea-stick and trusting to the binding of raffia to hold the handle
firmly. When this is done, the rope need not be quite so long as when
it is twisted. We have, also, dyed the mop occasionally. If dipped in
red or green ink, the hairs look particularly attractive, especially when
green or red raffia is used for the binding.

A LONG SNAKE

Some folk think that snakes are horrid creatures. Personally, we find
the unpoisonous ones very pleasant companions, and we ought to know
because we have more than forty in a cage. But what we really wanted
to say about snakes is this. Have you ever made one? Not one that
stings, of course. Never? Well, this is the way. When letters come
to your house, take off the stamps and peel away the paper backing so
that the perforations stick out. You will want several hundreds, but
they need not be all the same colour, so put them away safely in a box
until you have enough. Your friends and relations may be willing to
help you to get all you want, but why not ask your father to bring some
home occasionally from the office?

When you have a large heap, pierce each one in the middle and thread
it on a piece of tough, thin string, or linen thread. Make a knot at one
end of the string and add the stamps at the other end by means of a
needle, which should go through the centre of each stamp. Put them

on at any angle, so that the coil is more or less tubular.   When the coil is about 2 feet long, add no more stamps, but get a large Brazil nut ; ask your brother to cut off a third of it with his fret-saw, pick out the edible part and give it to your brother for his trouble and bore a hole through the tip of the shell.   Put the string through this hole and force the shell up to the stamps.   Knot the string tightly and cut off the unwanted part.   If you decorate the shell to look like a snake's head, you will have a very real-looking reptile which won't sting and won't need feeding as ours do.   Of course, you must only use very common stamps.   It would be a sin to put holes through rare ones.

A USEFUL BOX-SEAT

It is a bad plan to have too many things in the bedroom, but a certain number of articles are necessary for comfort.   Here is an attractive makeshift piece of furniture, which most girls will find useful.   Obtain a well-made wooden box from the grocer.

Let it be long for its width and depth.   Go over it carefully and see

A Suggested
Arrangement for your
Bedroom Window.

that there are no stray nails on which to catch the fingers and clothes. Then stand it on its side and fit four squat feet, so as to raise it slightly from the ground.   Round wooden drawer handles will prove just the thing, and they can be bought for a few pence from such stores as Woolworth's.   Now cover the top and three sides with cretonne, fixing the material in position with boot nails. Pad the top, if desired, with any accumulation of rags that may be handy. Put a curtain frill on the open side of the box. You will now have a useful box-seat in which you can keep your footwear or anything that tends to make your room look untidy.

A KITCHEN UTENSIL HOLDER

" Where's the tin-opener ? " and " What has happened to the cork-screw ? " These are remarks often overheard in the kitchen. The reason why the tin-opener and cork-screw have the habit of becoming elusive the moment they are wanted is that they are usually kept huddled together, with an assortment of similar things, and one helps to hide the other.

A really good plan is to take a piece of gingham or printed cotton, about 20 inches square, to sew over the edges and to fix rows of little pockets, each one of which is reserved for a special article. Naturally, two loops must be sewn to the upper edge, so that the square may hang snugly on the kitchen wall.

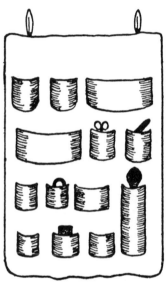

Do not make the pockets too deep or the articles put in them will be difficult to get out. Also, it helps in locating a thing, if it can be partly seen. It will be a good plan to provide pockets of various sizes.

A Kitchen Utensil Holder   An Egg Cosy

AN EGG COSY

Felt is used for various purposes in furnishing. If you happen to have some small pieces left over, and they are of attractive colours, why not make one or two egg cosies ? They are very useful little things, and they will make all the difference between a cold egg and one fit to eat, when you happen to come down to breakfast a few minutes late.

For each cosy you will need three pieces of felt, cut to a domed shape, as shown in the illustration. The extreme height should be about 3 inches, and the bottom edge, 2½ inches. The sides should be gently curved. Sew the three pieces together along the sides with a buttonhole stitch, and cut the bottom edges into points, as shown.

You do not want the felt too thick, and if you are able to select the material, choose three different colours to make up each cosy, unless you want them to accord with some colour scheme which you have in mind.

A SCULLERY TIDY

Do you want to give someone a useful present or make something for a bazaar that does not cost much ? If so, here is the very thing.

Go to one of the cheap stores and buy the following articles : (1) a wooden spoon, for stirring saucepans, (2) a dish mop, with a nice white fluffy head, (3) a small check duster, (4) a washing-up dish cloth, made of net, and (5) a piece of house flannel, about a foot square.

On the back of the bowl of the spoon, paint or draw a face, bearing some grotesque or funny expression. Behind the spoon, arrange the mop so that it looks like white hairs, fringing the face. Wrap the net over the hairs, to appear as though it were a shawl. Then, fold the duster in halves, diagonally, and place the long edge round the shoulders of the curious creature. Lastly, tie the house flannel around the waist to serve as a skirt and to keep the various items together. The creature is as useful as it is funny.

A KITCHEN RUG

Do mother a good turn in two ways—make her a kitchen rug and empty her rag bag ! She will appreciate both kindnesses.

The only materials required are (1) a wooden skewer, (2) a piece of canvas cut to the size of the rug desired, (3) a piece of stout material, such as coarse calico, of the same dimensions as the rug, for lining, (4) and the *woollen* rags accumulated for years. The more varied the colour of these rags the better. Anything will do, old stockings, old serge curtains, table covers, etc.

The first step is to lay in a stock of these rags, cut to the size required. This may be done during any odd moments in the day. When a fair supply is prepared, then it is time to start on the rug itself. The rags must be cut into strips, roughly 1 inch wide by 4 inches long ; do not cut them straight across at each end, but diagonally. This prevents the threads from fraying.

Now decide on the size of the rug and cut the canvas accordingly, allowing an extra margin of $1\frac{1}{2}$ inches at every edge for turning in and possible fraying.

It will be found much more convenient to work, if the canvas is stretched over a frame. There is no need to buy one for the purpose ; an ordinary airing clothes-horse will prove quite an efficient substitute. Your particular clothes-horse may be a two-leaf or three-leaf variety ; it does not matter which it is, as only one leaf will be needed, and it may be shut up and laid down flat. You will probably find that the canvas does not exactly fit over the section of the horse. Arrange it so that one edge may be secured, either by means of drawing pins or tacks to one wooden side, then draw the canvas across to the opposite side and secure it in the same way. If the whole length or width of the rug exactly fits this frame, so much the better. If it does not, then the work must be done in sections, the portion under treatment being stretched tightly on the frame as described above.

It is necessary to have easy access to both sides of the work at once, so do not lay the frame flat on a table ; if you do, you will find that the whole will have to be lifted when you want to work on the underneath side. Place one end of the horse on the edge of the kitchen table and lay the opposite end either on the edge of the dresser, or support it on the backs of two chairs, thus making a bridge. This enables you to work on the top and under sides of the rug without having to turn the whole arrangement over.

You may decide to have a plain border of several inches all round the rug, filling the centre with irregular jazz colourings. If so, work the border first. Start at the lower right hand corner, and with the wooden skewer punch a hole in the canvas ; now punch another hole half an inch to the left of the first one ; take a strip of rag of the colour desired for the border, and with the skewer push one end down through the first hole ; draw the strip down till about $1\frac{1}{2}$ inches remain above, then push the lower end up through the second hole. You now have two ends of a rag strip sticking up on the same side of the rug.

Now punch two more holes in a straight line with the first two, and proceed as before with another strip of the same colour. Do this along the whole length of the rug and repeat for six or eight rows for the border. Continue these rows along each of the four sides, and then work the middle part, backwards and forwards, with rags of all colours, so that the centre is a mass of colour.

When the whole canvas is completely threaded with coloured strips, turn the edges in, about one inch all round, and oversew securely to a strong lining, along each side. This makes a cosy kitchen rug at practically no cost.

A USEFUL DOYLEY CASE

You have probably been annoyed some time or other by the persistent way in which doyleys manage to get themselves creased and soiled-looking, in spite of the fact that they have probably not been used since they were last laundered. To put them away neatly with the best linen appears to be quite useless. They still become crumpled, and when a particular one is wanted, it is almost invariably unfit for appearing on a table.

If a doyley case is used you will find that all further trouble is at an end.

You need two pieces of firm cardboard, large enough to give two rounds, each 9 inches in diameter. A case of this size will take doyleys large enough for a bread plate.

Procure some attractive material, either flowered silk, voile, or cretonne and plain white muslin or silk for a lining.

Cut two rounds of cretonne and two of plain white material, each just a shade larger than the cardboard rounds. Turn in the edges very narrowly, place the white lining on one side of a cardboard circle and the flowered material on the other side and stitch the two pieces of material together firmly. A neat finish is given by binding the edge with a narrow

Q

ribbon, gathering it slightly all round, as is sometimes done to the brims of hats.

Do exactly the same with the other piece of cardboard.

Join these two stiff covers together with hinges made of ribbon, long enough to allow room for 12 or 15 doyleys between the covers.

On the opposite side to the hinges fasten two pieces of wide ribbon to match the hinges and binding ribbon. Keep the covers closed by tying these in a large bow.

PAPER DOYLEYS

There are a hundred uses for paper doyleys in the kitchen. You can make really attractive ones quite easily. Fold a sheet of paper first into two, then two again, and once more into two. This will give you a

shape like that in the illustration. Then make cuts as indicated by the black spaces. Open out and you have an excellent doyley for a cake dish or a number of other things. Note that circular doyleys, the most useful shape of all, are made by folding in squares and curving the outside edge of the folded paper.

MARKING YOUR LINEN

Many people find it a great bother to mark their linen properly. All sorts of little troubles arise, and as often as not the name, when it is written, is an eyesore. But really the work is quite simple if done in the following way. First of all, do not use the broad quill pen which is supplied with some brands of marking ink. Only an expert could hope to be satisfied with it. Use rather a new steel nib, and throw it away when the batch of marking is done. Take the article to be branded and wrap it tightly round a flat ruler, so that the place where the name is to be written is on the upper surface of the ruler.

The material must be perfectly level, and without creases. If thought desirable, pencil lines to indicate the heights of the letters.

Do not write, but print in capitals. Do not have the nib full of ink. Make all the strokes downwards. Place the index finger and thumb

```
ABCDEFGHIJKLMNO
PQRSTUVWXYZ
1234567890
abcdefghijklmnopqrst
uvwxyz.
Mary  Ethel . Gladys 'Diana .
Amy . Joan . Bertha . Catherine .
Winifred . Freda . Hilda . Irene .
Louisa . Nora . Phyllis . Rose .
Sybil . Thelma . Victoria .
```

Suggestions for Lettering when Marking Linen.

of the left hand just above and below the spot where each letter is to be printed. If you mark your linen in this way you will not experience any trouble.

A RADIATOR COVER FOR THE CAR

Have you ever seen your father or brother try to swing over the engine of his car in the cold weather? It is one of those things that makes him vow that he will never take the car out again except when the weather is tropical. Now, there is really no need for the engine to cool right down in cold weather and if it is just a little warm it will start up fairly easily. The thing is to wrap up the radiator with a sort of tea-cosy. You have probably seen cars running about with them on.

Why not make one of these very useful articles? The work is not difficult if you know the measurements. You will want the length from A to B, also from A to C, and you must know what fittings there are at D and their position. The length from B to E should be roughly 6 inches.

Having obtained the dimensions, it will be advisable to cut a paper pattern and work from it. Remember that all the measurements you take are inside lengths; outside figures will be generally 2 inches more.

Any black material will do for the inner face of the cover. On this should be stitched wadding, purchased at six-three a yard, and the outside ought to be American cloth, black or dark brown. Real leather would, of course make a far better job, but it is too expensive.

If the car carries a mascot, or an AA badge at the head, a hole must be arranged in the cosy to enable it to be slipped over. Also, it will be advisable to arrange a roll-up flap in the front, to allow the radiator to be exposed when desirable. Both sides of this roll-up blind should be covered with American cloth, and two small straps and buckles ought to be provided so that it can be held tightly. When the blind is down, the straps should fit into two more buckles, so that the wind cannot blow it about. Another and larger strap and buckle should be fitted at E, then under the bonnet, to a point opposite to E. This will keep the cover from slipping off.

Any motoring friend will be glad of one of these radiator covers. It will save lots of trouble, and, after all, it is not very hard nor expensive to make.

MAKING BATH SALTS

Some people regard bath salts as an unnecessary luxury and a waste of money. As a matter of fact, the use of a handful of these crystals renders the water slightly alkaline and neutralises the lime, both of which are good for the skin.

To make a supply of bath salts, take two or three pounds of good washing soda and roll it so as to crush all the large lumps. Now put it, by handfuls, in a sieve, and so separate the powder from the crystals. When all has been so treated, put the powder with the kitchen supply, as it is no use for the present purpose, and spread the crystals out on several thicknesses of newspaper and put into a warm oven. Turn them over occasionally. When warm and dry, place them in your washing bowl, previously washed and dried, and pour over them some essence of lavender and mix well. Use a quarter of an ounce of the essence for each pound of crystals. As quickly as possible, store in wide-mouthed stoppered bottles, or air-tight tins. Any desired scent can be substituted for the lavender.

HOW TO MAKE YOUR OWN SMELLING SALTS

Another easy-to-make present for your friend's birthday. You will find numbers of small scent bottles, which have been finished with, lying about the house, and the smelling salts to go in them are easily made as follows :—

Inexhaustible Smelling Salts.—Take 8 drams of Sal tartar, 6 drams of granulated muriate of ammonia, 5 minims of oil of neroli, 5 minims of oil of lavender flowers, 3 minims of oil of rose, and 15 minims of spirits of ammonia. Put into the scent bottle to be used as a container a piece of sponge, filling about one quarter of the space, then pour on it the proper portion of the oils. After this put in the mixed salts, and then pour on the spirits of ammonia and securely cork the bottle.

The following recipes for volatile salts are easily made and these salts are always useful :—

1. One pint of Liquor of ammonia fort, 1 dram of oil of lavender flowers, 1 dram of oil of rosemary (fine), ½ dram of oil of bergamot, 10 minims of oil of peppermint. Mix these ingredients thoroughly together and keep in a well-corked bottle.

2. Ten ounces of Sesqui-carbonate and 5 ounces of concentrated liquor of ammonia. Put the Sesqui-carbonate in a wide-mouthed bottle. Perfume the liquor of ammonia to suit your requirements and then pour it over the carbonate. Put in a cool place and stir with a stiff spatula— *i.e.*, a tiny spade often used especially for this purpose—every other day for one week. Then keep well closed for a further fortnight, when it may be used freely.

THE BOBBING HEADS

All boys and girls are fascinated with water and like to play with it. Here is something that will provide a good deal of fun. Get the cork of

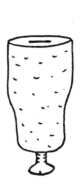

a wine-bottle and rub it up on a piece of glass-paper until it is nice and smooth as well as clean. Then cut a slit in the top edge and, on a piece of cardboard, draw a face with a neck attached. Force the neck into the cork-slit, and in the under edge drive a stout, stumpy nail.

Fill up the bath with water and float this little contrivance on the surface. The nail should steady the bobbing head ; but if it pulls it under the water it is too heavy and a lighter one must replace it.

The head may represent some grotesque person or any animal, such as a duck swimming or a cat that has had the misfortune to fall into the water. Why not make half a dozen different bobbers ?

Ordinary water-colours should not be used to ornament the faces, as they will run. Waterproof inks are best for the purpose.

AN EASILY-MADE DOLL'S BUNGALOW

Years ago, when we used to play with our doll's house, we soon got tired because it involved so much stooping. Now here is something which we think is better than a doll's house ; it is a doll's bungalow. And as you can play with it on the nursery table you will neither have to stoop nor kneel.

To make the bungalow you will want some large pieces of cardboard.

For the floor get a sheet 24 inches square. For the walls take two pieces 24 inches long and 12 inches high. And for the roof another piece will be required a little larger than the floor piece.

The floor piece will need no shaping. The walls are easily planned.

Pencil a line across each of the two pieces so that they are both divided into two squares of 12 inches. Along the pencil line make a cut, in each, 6 inches long, starting from one edge. Stand the two pieces on the long edges at right angles, one with the cut below, the other with the cut above. You will see that the cuts enable the two cards to slip one within the other, and they stand firmly on edge. Put these walls centrally on the floor card. Now for a roof.

Draw a pencil line along the middle of the card you have reserved for the roof, so that the line divides it into two spaces, 12 inches by 24 inches.

Run the tip of a pocket-knife along the line and cut half way, no more, through the card ; then bend the card along the score line. If this card be placed on the top of the walls it will be flat, and roofs are not usually flat. Therefore go back to the walls, take one of the cards, not both, and pencil a line, I inch from the top of the two outside edges, and slope it up to the top of the card in the centre. Cut along the line, refit the card into the companion wall card, stand it on the floor and lift on the roof, which will now slope down nicely.

The building is now up, but a lot of little things remain to be done. You will want some doors. In the four walls cut openings, 5 inches by 3 inches, and hinge on the cut-out portions by means of adhesive tape. Cover the ceilings with white paper. Paste wallpaper on to the walls, and stick little pictures here and there. Get some tile papers out of an old catalogue for the floor. Paint the roof to imitate slates or tiles, draw panels on the doors, and in every way you can make the rooms look cosy. Your doll's furniture will, of course, fill the rooms.

Do not forget that when you have done playing, the whole of the bungalow should be taken to pieces and packed flat.

HOW TO MAKE A KNIFE CLEANER FOR THE DOLL'S HOUSE

Have you a knife-cleaner for your Dolly ? Why not ?—nothing is easier to make. First hunt out two small round boxes—the lids of gas mantle boxes will serve the purpose well. Fix them together as in the illustration and bend a hairpin for the handle. Then stick the latter

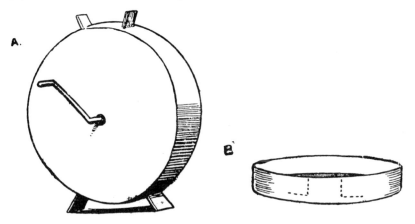

KNIFE CLEANER FOR DOLL'S HOUSE.

right through the middle of the boxes, turning the end over so that it cannot fall out. The sketch will show you. Next fix the stands for the knives on top by gumming on two bits of matches.

To make the knife cleaner stand firmly, cut the outer lid where indicated by the dotted lines on the sketch, and bend the two pieces back to form the supports.

Now it is complete, and you make Dolly a present of it for her house. She will bring out her knives and will commence to clean them.

THE CAT IN THE CHICKEN HOUSE

Of course, you know that cats ought not to be allowed in chicken houses ; but we are going to have one, just for fun. First of all, take a piece of stout drawing paper and rule an even number of lines with equi-distant spaces between them. By way of an example, rule fourteen vertical lines, each 2½ inches long and ⅜ of an inch apart. Enclose all these lines by ruling two other lines, one at the top and one at the bottom of them. Now, this will give you thirteen spaces. In order that you shall make no mistake, just scribble on the even spaces, *i.e.*, 2, 4, 6, 8, 10 and 12. Place the paper on a flat card or piece of glass, and, with a sharp pocket knife and ruler, cut out the spaces scribbled on. You are beginning to see the idea now. What we have is the series of bars for the chicken house.

The next thing is to pencil a line all round the bars making the space an inch wide. This completes the front of the house. But you will want sides, chiefly because the front has to stand up. So, make side flaps to stand as a screen does. Cut the front and sides out, and fold back the sides. Stand it up. If it is shaky and flimsy, glue two thin strips of card along to the very top and bottom of the front. That will give it strength.

Now, spread the paper out flat on the table, and underneath it put a clean sheet of drawing paper. You will be able to see part of it through the bars. Take a sharp pencil and just glide it along the cut-out edges. Lift up the house and you will find six enclosed spaces with five others between them, making eleven in all, on the under sheet. Draw another line at which end you please, but make it ⅜ of an inch away from the nearest line. This will give you a total of twelve spaces. Cut along the top, bottom and extreme outside lines.

You now have to bring your artistic talent into play. In spaces 1, 3, 5, 7, 9 and 11, you draw and paint a cat, and in spaces 2, 4, 6, 8, 10 and 12 you draw a number of frightened chickens. The best way to do this is to take the house with the bars and place it face down so that the bars cover the even spaces. You can now draw the cat on the bars as well as in the spaces. When that is done, shift the house so that the bars cover the odd spaces, and then draw the chickens on the bars as well as in the spaces. The bars will look rather curious but it will not matter, as it is the back that you have been defacing. We suggested this method because it helps you to get the shapes properly distanced.

Lift up the bars and paint the two sectional pictures, and when they are dry, cut a length of thin card, ½ an inch wide and 7 inches long. Glue it horizontally to the back of the sectional pictures, somewhere in the middle, and cut two slots, one at either end of the sides of the front of the house. Place the cat and the chickens behind the bars, slip the projecting ends of the card through the slots, stand the chicken house up and your little contrivance is finished. Pull one of the projections to the left and we have the chickens in view ; pull the handle to the right and the cat comes to light.

THE CHANGING INDIVIDUAL

This is an idea that used to be very popular years ago but which is not often indulged in to-day. You take a piece of paper cut to the shape shown. Each space in our case is a square, but any rectangular shape will do equally well. The only thing is that each space must be exactly the same size. Crease the paper along the dotted lines and cut it where the full lines are shown.

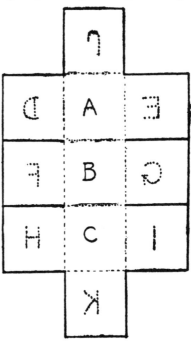

Now draw in the spaces A, B and C the figure of a person. The head, alone, comes in space A, the trunk and arms in B and the legs in C.

Next, fold D over A and draw a totally different head; but see that it fits on to the body B. Do the same with E.

When that is done, fold F over B and draw a different body to fit the head A, and the legs C. Do similarly with G.

Spaces H and I are used for supplying different legs.

Fold space J over A and give it yet another head; then fold K over C and provide more legs.

By flapping different pieces over the main body, you have a large number of distinct individuals. Note particularly that A, B and C are drawn on the front of the paper, all the others on the back; also that J and K must be placed upside down.

SHAPES AND FORMS IN NUMBERS

Here is a funny-looking motor car, but the look of it is not what we are thinking about just now. What we want to know is how much is the most it adds up to? That's a funny question to ask, perhaps, but

if you look carefully you will see that every line is part of a figure. This suggests a good game. Ask your friends, when they are round at your house, to make pictures composed of nothing but figures. Letters will do equally well. And then, somebody else must add up all the figures and find the total. Common objects should be selected, with not too many lines. In the case of letters, they must be set out in alphabetical arrangement. Where a letter or figure has two identities, according to the way it is viewed, make it a rule that the higher value of the figure is counted and the earlier letter in the alphabet is accepted.

THE HANDKERCHIEF DOLL

Take a clean handkerchief and spread it out flat. Then tightly roll up one of the long sides until the middle is reached, and follow by rolling up the other side until the two rolls lie side by side (Fig. A).

Next take the farther end of the two rolls and double them over, so that they almost, but not quite, touch the nearer end (Fig. B).

After that, bend the nearer end under the end just folded (Fig. C).

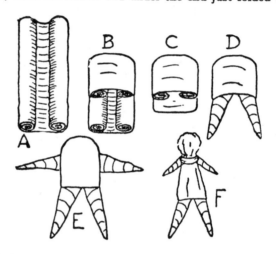

When this is done, press on the handkerchief with one hand and with the other search for the two corners, which will be found one in each roll, and pull downwards (Fig. D).

Follow by finding the two other ends of the handkerchief and pull them outwards and sidewards (Fig. E).

Tie these two latter ends around the mass of handkerchief, an inch from the end (Fig. F), and you have an attractive doll—all made in a minute.

NIGHTMARE FACES

Nobody wants a nightmare, but nightmare faces are something worth having. Get one or two old kid gloves that are white. Those your mother used to wear with evening dress will do nicely, as long as she does not want them any more. Cut off the fingers about 1½ inches from the tips, and slip them one by one on the first finger of the right hand. Whilst there, take some Indian ink and draw the most terrible faces you can devise on the soft leather. Then get out your paint box and add patches of colour—red, yellow, green, etc.—to the cheeks, neck, and so on. By snipping the leather, you can provide your monstrosities with long, lopping ears, and if you cut little rings out of the unwanted parts of the glove, you will be able to make neck frills and other adornments for your beasts.

When the heads have dried, slip one or two on the fingers of each hand. It will be good fun in making them fight and do all sorts of antics.

THE RING OF DANCERS

Take a sheet out of an exercise book which has the usual blue lines on it. Crease every second line in a zig-zag way, as shown in the first diagram, and then cut off a piece about an inch wide. The remainder of the folded paper will do for further attempts.

On the top fold of the strip, draw a man, a woman, an animal, or almost anything you choose, but be careful that the object touches both side edges of the paper. Now, take a pair of scissors and cut out your drawing, cutting not only the top fold, but all of them at the same time. Hold the paper firmly while you do the cutting.

When this is done, unbend the paper, and you will see that you have one long strip of people or things. Bend them in a circle, dab a smear of paste on the two ends and so join them, as shown in the second figure. Our quaint ladies are supposed to be getting ready for a game of " Ring-a-ring-of-Roses."

THE PIG'S TAIL

Most pigs are very uninteresting creatures, but this little fellow is different. He will provide you with no end of fun if you treat him kindly. Draw his outline on a large sheet of white paper and mark off the numbered sections, as we have indicated. Do not, on any account, draw his tail, but cut out a little twirly thing of paper and put a pin through the end farthest from the tip.

Now, you remember the old game at parties of trying to fix the tail in the right place when you were blindfolded? Well, this is better than that. What you do is to collect three or four friends, blindfold them

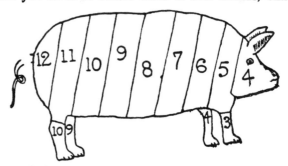

one by one, and they take turns to see who can score forty points. The nearer you get to the right spot, the more you count and that is where all the fun comes in.

It is not a bad idea to colour the sections of the pig. He will then look something like a glorified zebra.

WHAT DO THE FATES SAY?

You know how the people in olden days used to consult the oracle? Well, here is a little oracle that you can make for yourself. Do not cut out the two circles, but draw larger circles with a compass and make them of stiff drawing paper. Note that there are twelve sections in each circle. You can easily divide up the circumferences into these sections, because the radius of a circle will mark off six times on the outer ring of a circle and, when you have marked off the six sections, it will be no trouble at all to halve them. It is not necessary to copy the questions and answers we have given. Make up your own set if you like: but mind that every question must permit of the answer " yes " or " no." Colour each section if you choose ; that will make the oracle look smart.

When all the drawing and cutting has been done, put a big pin through the centre of the small circle, and then push it through the centre of the larger one. Finally, fix it into a door or any firm piece of upright wood.

The oracle is ready to do its work. Ask it one of the questions and then spin the wheels round. When they come to rest, you have the answer.

As we cannot think of all the questions you would like to ask the fates, we have left four spaces blank, but they are numbered. Suppose you want to know whether so and so will invite you to tea? Decide on the question and then choose one of the numbers, say 4. When the wheels finish spinning, your answer will be opposite to number 4.

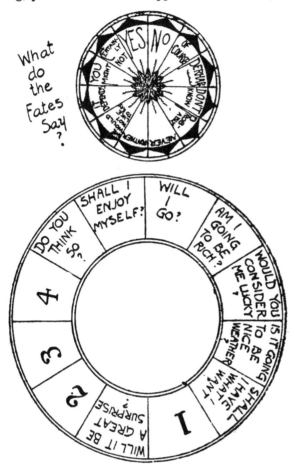

Note that the spaces will seldom overlap exactly when they stop turning. What counts is where the pointers come to rest.

Of course, it is only a bit of fun, and, after all, the answers may be entirely wrong.

CAN YOU WALK THROUGH A POST-CARD

Of course you cannot. The thing seems quite impossible. Nevertheless, we can soon show you how to do so, and then you will be able to put the problem to your friends and amaze them.

Take an ordinary post-card and cut it across the middle, as shown in A. Be careful not to cut right to the edges ; in fact leave about half an inch at both ends.

Now make from seven to a dozen cuts from both the top and bottom sides towards the centre cut ; but do not let any of them reach the horizontal slit. See diagram B.

Third, make interior vertical cuts as shown in C. Arrange them

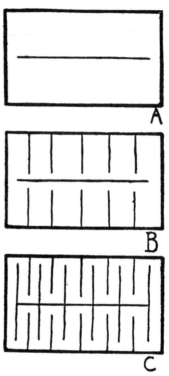

alternately between those already shown in B. See that these fresh cuts do not reach the top and bottom edges of the card.

You have now done all the cutting that is necessary, and the card will open out and form a ring easily large enough for you to walk through.

THE BOAT THAT WILL ALWAYS FLOAT

You know how small kiddies love to play with things that will float, when they are having a bath. Here is a capital idea to please them. Take a cork from an empty wine bottle and cut it down the centre length-wise. You immediately have the body for two tiny boats. But trim the ends of the cork in each case and a still more realistic ship will be revealed to you. Sails will be wanted, so cut them out of an old stiff white collar belonging to your father. Do not have them too big or too high, as the lower the boats are rigged, the less chance they will have of toppling over. Draw the masts and the ropes on the sails in fixed Indian ink ; it will not run in the water then. To fix the sails, just cut a longitudinal slit down the centre of each deck and slip an edge of the sail into it. The cork will grip it tightly and keep it in place. You can make two of these boats in three minutes, but they will amuse a kiddie for a considerably longer time.

A SMART ROCKING HORSE

This is not a bad little article. Obtain a cork from an empty wine bottle and then a piece of springy card. Let the latter be 6 inches long and 1 inch wide. The cork serves for the body of the horse and the card is curved to act as the rocker. Pin the ends of the card to the ends of the cork, as shown. Let the pins at the back hold on a tail made of

some short lengths of wool knotted together. Black a patch on the cork as shown, to serve as a saddle. Cut the head out of card and paint it " dappled-grey." Slip it in position by making a deep slit in the cork with a pocket knife. Three or four of these lively creatures will amuse young children for hours.

If pieces of thin tin are used instead of the card, the horses will enjoy a much longer life.

AN ATTRACTIVE SKIPPING ROPE

Buy a ball of nice string and cut from it a dozen to eighteen pieces, each three yards long. Dip some of the lengths in red ink, others in green, others again in blue-black ink, and the remainder in different coloured inks if you have any.

When all are tinted, hang them over a line to dry; but see that if they drip no harm will be caused.

As soon as they are quite dry plait them together and so form an attractively coloured rope.

For handles, bind some electrician's tape or adhesive plaster along 4 inches from each end of the rope, and then cover this by winding some coloured string round and round the tape or plaster, in the same way that the handle of a cricket bat is formed. The tape keeps the binding string from coming undone.

If you prefer a rather thick handle, use a good deal of tape before the string is bound round it.

A TOY DOVE-COTE

Here is an admirable toy dove-cote, for when you play with your models on the table. Take two empty reels, preferably of the fat, squat shape, such as is used for silk. Also, procure a piece of thin card and cut from it two squares, having sides of two inches. Next, take a cheap penholder that does not taper in the handle. Now force an end of the handle in one of the reels and give it just a touch of liquid glue to keep it there. Take one of the square cards, pierce the centre, and push it on the penholder so that it drops down on to the reel. This makes the foot of the dove-cote.

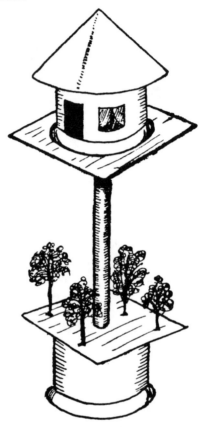

To construct the cote itself, stand the penholder upright, pierce the second card in the middle and drop it on the holder. Follow it with the second reel and glue the two together. Push them on to the handle of the penholder so that the latter comes half an inch above the top of the reel. Now shape out a circle of paper, 3 inches in diameter and cut a radius line. This will enable you to twist the circle into a cone, and the overlapping part is stuck down. This shape is then dropped on to the top reel and when glued there serves admirably for a sloping roof. Paint the roof a bright brick red and the top reel white, but add a black door and window. The upper platform should be brown and the lower one green. Choose any bright colour for the bottom reel. If you care to do so, push little twigs out of the garden into the lower platform to look like bushes.

MAKING A CANDLE CLOCK

Have you ever told the time with the assistance of a burning candle ? The history books tell us that King Arthur used candles for the purpose. His method was surprisingly accurate, though we should not like to have to catch trains by it. Here is his plan.

First of all, obtain half a dozen candles all of the same make and size. Hard, slow-burning ones will serve us best. Next, light one of them and place it out of all draught. When it has burnt for half an hour stand one of the unburnt candles by the side of it and mark, on the fresh candle, the height of the lighted candle. Do this every half hour until the candle has burnt away.

We now have a candle with marks showing the amount that will burn in half an hour. Divide the sections into lesser sections, and so provide five or ten minute sections. Colour the sections alternately red and blue or any other tints you fancy, and number them, beginning at the top, thus, 10, 20, 30, 40, etc., to 1 hr., 1 hr. 10, 1 hr. 20, etc. Place the remaining candles by the side of the marked one and treat them all alike.

NOTE.—When lighting a clock candle note the actual time, and add it to whatever time is indicated by the section marks.

A BEAUTIFUL KALEIDOSCOPE

A kaleidoscope is a marvellous instrument, which provides millions of pretty geometric patterns with not the slightest trouble. You can make one of these things for about a shilling, and it will give you hours of enjoyment.

First, go into the kitchen and hunt around until you find an empty

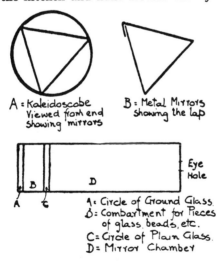

A = Kaleidoscope Viewed from end showing mirrors

B = Metal Mirrors showing the lap

Eye Hole

A = Circle of Ground Glass.
B = Compartment for Pieces of glass, beads, etc.
C = Circle of Plain Glass.
D = Mirror Chamber

cylindrical tin. If you have a choice, pick a tall one with as small a circular end as you can. We recently used a two-pound coffee tin, and it served the purpose admirably. Having obtained the tin, we stood it upside down with the lid on and punched a hole through the bottom end. This hole we opened out to the size of a halfpenny, by pushing a wide screwdriver through and twisting it round. Rough edges on the outside were filed off : those inside were ignored.

The first part was easily done. Next, we removed the lid, and taking some stiff card, bent it into a long three-sided tunnel. It was shaped so that the tunnel could be wedged just tight enough to fit into the tin without slipping round. Diagram A shows how the arrangement looked when viewed from the top. Note that the three sides of the triangle are as nearly equal as could be obtained.

While the bent card was in position, we noted how far it reached up the tin. We did not want it to come any nearer the top than an inch. So, carefully lifting out the card from the tin, we cut enough off the length to make it just right. Now, the card itself is of no use for the kaleidoscope, it is merely a pattern. This pattern we used for shaping a piece of sheet tin. The tin must have a good polished surface, and as this surface is apt to become dull in time, it is better to make the triangle of three pieces of glass, backed with black paper. But this, however, is a refinement that is not really necessary.

The tin being fitted into position in place of the card, we placed on top of it a flat circle of plain clear glass, which a glazier cut for us for twopence. Then, around the inside of the tin, and standing on this circle of glass, we fitted a collar of cardboard. And on top of this collar, we fitted another flat circle of glass, but this one was made of ground glass.

Before placing this last circle in position, we collected a few small glass beads, two or three tiny pieces of coloured glass, and a number of other small transparent, coloured articles. They were dropped into the compartment between the two rounds of glass.

To hold the top glass in place, we bound all round the edge with passe-partout slips. The kaleidoscope was complete, but to give it a finish, we pasted some brown leatherette paper round the circular side and a ring of it on the " eye " end.

To enjoy this little instrument, hold it up to the light and place an eye to the hole at the bottom. A beautiful geometric pattern is seen. A little tilt of the tin, and a different pattern reveals itself.

A NOAH'S ARK

Every child will want a Noah's Ark at some period or other in its juvenile career. We have made several at various times, by request, for youngsters of our acquaintance. And to tell the truth, they are rather fidgety things to make if constructed on the usual lines. There are so many sharp angles and curves to complicate the work. Experience, however, has taught us a few tricks which enable us now to make a Noah's Ark with far more ease than formerly.

Here are the suggestions we have to make. Obtain a cardboard box, about 8 by 4 inches, and 5 inches deep. Cut half-way down the four corners. Then cut along the two long sides from the bottom of the corner cuts. Now cut the short ends to a point. All this may be rather complicated to follow from the wording, but a glance at the illustration will make everything clear in a moment.

The shape, so obtained, serves as the four walls of the house. Cut a piece of card to act as roof. Let it be at least an inch longer than the box and sufficiently wide to overhang the sides. Arrange it over the cut-out box, and stick it in position by fixing long lengths of narrow pasted paper in the angles.

To make the boat part of the ark, obtain another cardboard box, larger than the first. Stand it upside down with the lid off. Put the house part centrally on it, as shown in the illustration, and glue the two

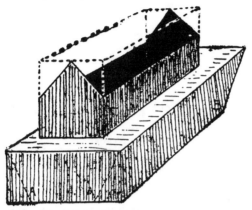

together. Now cut the four corners, as indicated by the dotted line A, and when that has been effected, push the sides under so that they slant inwards, as shown at B. A paper fastener will keep each corner secure. Trim away the edges as required. The lower box now looks like a barge and the whole has much the appearance of Noah's temporary abode.

What remains to be done is straightforward. Cover the whole shape with clean paper, including a stout piece underneath. Then paint the roof red, the walls leave alone, but draw doors and windows and colour them blue and green. Lastly, paint the boat a rich brown.

TOY SCALES

Here is a very simple way to make a nice pair of toy scales, suitable

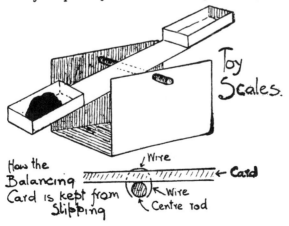

Toy Scales.

How the Balancing Card is kept from Slipping

Wire ← Card

Wire
Centre rod

for when a small girl is playing shops.   Hunt out from the store-room an empty cardboard box.   The exact dimensions do not much matter ; but about 4 by 3 inches will be a very serviceable size.

Take the box and carefully cut out the two short ends.   Through the middle of each long side, close up to the top edge, pierce a hole and push the handle of a penholder from one opening to the other.   This will make a horizontal bridge, running across the box.

The next thing is to take a strip of cardboard, about 5 inches long by 1 inch wide.   At each end, glue the tray of an empty match-box.

The scales are complete.   By resting the long strip of card on the penholder bridge, you will be able to weigh small quantities of materials. For weights, use little strips of thick card.

THE PLAY-ROOM KIOSK

There are very few boys and girls who do not enjoy playing at shops. Below we describe the making of an attractive kiosk which will give hours and hours of amusement.

Take some long lengths of wood 2 inches by 1 inch in section.   Cut two strips each 4 feet long, and four strips 2 feet long.   With them make

a frame, using the long pieces for the horizontals.   Two of the short pieces will supply the vertical sides and the other two are put parallel to these sides, but one foot away from them.   Thus the frame is partitioned off into three spaces—(1) 1 foot by 2 feet ; (2) 2 feet by 2 feet ; and (3) 1 foot by 2 feet.   You may make the joins in any way you please ; but you will probably prefer to lap them or to use the " halving-joint " method, which makes a much neater job.

The next thing is to obtain three pieces of three-ply wood.   Two of them are to be 2 feet by 2 feet and one is to be 4 feet by 2 feet.   All round these pieces nail an edging of wood 1 inch in section.

Now spread out all the various sections on the floor, where you will have plenty of room.   First put a square three-ply panel at each short side of the skeleton frame, and arrange the other three-ply panel so that it touches one of the long sides.   Join all these pieces by means of hinges.

Can you see now that if the skeleton frame is stood up vertically on a table, and if the two side panels are placed at right angles to it, also if the long three-ply panel is turned over the top to make a roof, you have the shop part of a kiosk ?

Of course there are all sorts of little things that still need to be done if you want a really attractive shop. Hooks or bolts arranged inside will steady the structure and stop it falling down if knocked or pushed. Glass in two of the front openings will add a touch of realism ; but, of course, none should be fitted to the middle space, as that is where the customers are served. Behind the glass arrange shelves, so that you may display attractively the wares that you sell. Also a pot of paint will brighten things up a good deal. As you will be impatient and want to get the job finished, use a quick-drying cellulose paint. It will be hard in two hours.

The beauty of this kiosk is that it is so nice and big that you can sit in it when it is stood up on the play-room table, and best of all, it shuts up almost flat.

SHUTTLECOCKS

To make a serviceable shuttlecock, obtain a piece of close grained cork,

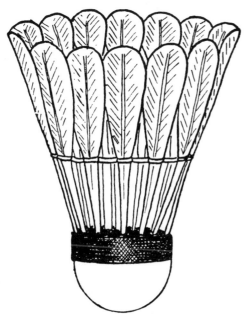

about an inch cube, and trim it with your pocket-knife so that it assumes the shape of a little more than half a sphere. Then, round the flat face, make a ring of twelve to fourteen holes with a knitting-needle. Be careful how you do this because it is very easy to split the cork. If this happens, do not throw away the shape, but glue the broken pieces together.

Then, obtain some feathers with strong quills. Your mother will be able to supply these next time she plucks a chicken. Take the feathers that seem most suitable and trim them with scissors, so that the feathery part is a little longer than the unclothed quill. Cut off the top in a nice curve and trim away the loose feathers at the base of the quill.

Now, put a drop of glue in each of the holes in the cork and force a quill in each hole. Lap the feathers, one over the other, as shown in the diagram, and make them all lean outwards. At the top, they should form a ring, much wider than at the base.

The last step is to bind the feathers together with a piece of fine string, at the point where the quills commence, making a loop round each. A band of tape, glued to the cork, completes the shuttle.

THE PAPER WINDMILL

You know those windmills with curly sails of coloured paper which hawkers sell in market places. Would you like to make one? It is quite easy. Cut a circle, about 9 inches across, out of some bright coloured paper. Stiff wall-paper will do admirably. Then make four slits, as shown in the lower diagram. Be careful that they do not come

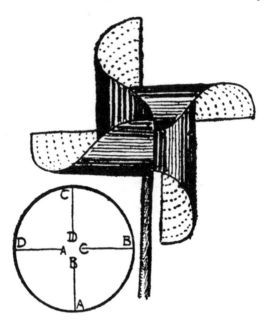

closer to the centre than half an inch. When you have done this, fold over the sections to make the curly sails. This is rather a fidgety business, but if you make sure of lapping A, on the circumference, over A at the centre, and B on B, C on C, and D on D, you will have no difficulty. When the sections are folded, run a pin through all the thicknesses of paper and push the tip of it into the head of a thin strip of wood, and you have a charming windmill which will revolve in a giddy fashion.

A DOLL MADE IN ELEVEN MINUTES

Do you like making dolls? Here is one you can put together in eleven minutes out of odd pieces of material, such as two or three white handkerchiefs, an old black stocking, and a piece of black ribbon.

This is your time-table:

1.—Cutting off the foot of the stocking just above the heel, folding the leg part in half, tying cotton round, 2 inches from the fold, and plumping it up to make a head. 1 minute.

2.—Stuffing the body with rags and sewing up along the bottom of skirt. 2 minutes.

3.—Rolling up tightly, lengthways, the foot of the stocking, tying in several places with cotton, and stitching it across the chest of the doll to serve as arms. 2 minutes.

4.—Cutting large white diamond out of handkerchief, making hole in centre, to slip over head, and sewing under the arms and down the sides. Trimming to shape where necessary. 2 minutes.

5.—Wrapping strip of a handkerchief round head and finishing it off in a bow at front. 1 minute.

6.—Putting on black waist-band, using a piece of black ribbon for the purpose. ½ minute.

7.—Making eyes, nose and mouth by sewing with white cotton. 2½ minutes.

Total, 11 minutes

DOLL

Take an old black stocking with no holes in it ; cut off the foot and heel and sew up the opening.   Then stuff it tightly with paper shavings, such as are found in chocolate boxes.   About 4 inches down tie a piece of red ribbon and pull it tightly so that it constricts the stocking and forms the neck.

Now turn to the open end of the stocking, cut two slits that run up about half its remaining length, and sew up nearly the whole of the two open sides. Use more paper shavings, and when the whole of the body and legs are rammed tightly, finish sewing up the open edges.

Next turn to the foot that was taken off and cut it so that, by the aid of a few stitches, it is transformed into two tubes that, when plumped out with shavings, will serve for arms. Sew these on to the body.

For the hair obtain some black wool, thread a needle with a long length, and then sew it a considerable number of times through the scalp ; but on each occasion leave a loop 2 inches long. When finished, cut the middle of each loop and thus make hairs 1 inch long. The eyes are provided by means of circles of coloured wool. The mouth and nose are worked in red wool—a long curved slit for the former and two little dots for the latter.

A short waistcoat may be added by sewing on a piece of red cloth, the buttons being two large bone buttons. Tie red ribbon near the end of the legs to shape the feet. The doll is complete.

BERTRAM THE BALL

It would be very difficult to say why Dismal Desmond, Mickey Mouse and all the other nursery characters have proved so popular; but, the reason hardly matters. Here, we have a novel suggestion. Why not sit down and invent an absolutely original character of your own and make him your mascot? What do you think of Bertram the Ball?

He's a plump little fellow, with large, inquisitive eyes, and his name is alliterative, as, of course, it should be.

Bertram can be made out of a soft piece of white velvet, stuffed to resemble a ball. His loppy ears are black velvet. His eyes, mouth and other features are all done by means of stitches. The bow, however, is a piece of ribbon, sewn down all round the edges.

Bertram makes a fine plaything for a small child. He should not be made too large or his owner will be unable to hug him comfortably.

A WOOLLY BALL FOR BABY

Have you ever wondered how your mother made those lovely big woolly balls when you were a tiny tot?

They are not at all difficult, and can be made easily in less than twenty minutes.

Collect all the various coloured wools which have been left over when making jumpers, and roll each colour into a small ball.

Now cut out two rounds exactly the same size from a sheet of cardboard. Decide first what size ball you want and cut the rounds accordingly. 3-inch circles would give one about the size of a tennis ball.

Then from the centre of each round cut out another circle of cardboard, about 1½ inches in diameter, thus making two cardboard rings about ¾ inch wide.

Take two strands of any colour wool, about 12 inches long, and place them together between the two rings. Be careful to see that the wool passes round the circumference of the cut-out circle ; do not let it cut across the middle of it. Keep the four ends of the strands together, well outside the rings.

Tie the rings together in three or four places with short pieces of wool, which are passed through the hole in the centre and tied on the outside

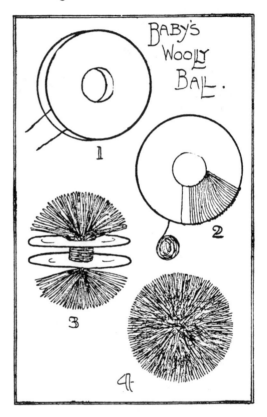

edge of the large circles. This keeps the cardboard firm and the two strands of wool in position between the two rings.

Now take one of the small balls of wool and begin to wind it round the rings thus : Hold the end of the wool firmly against the cardboard, pass the wool ball through the hole and over the outside edge of the cardboard ; draw the wool tightly and continue passing the ball through the middle and over the outside edge, gradually covering the cardboard entirely.

Take particular care to keep free the ends of the strands of wool which has been placed between the two rounds.

When all this ball has been wound, take one of another colour, and proceed in the same way, being careful to cover the cardboard evenly.

Do not wind the wool in ridges. Continue till the hole in the centre is nearly closed with wool.

Now begin to cut the wool at the outside edge. First take the loose strands which have been kept free firmly in the left hand, and with some sharp scissors cut through the wool at the extreme outside of the cardboard rounds. Work very carefully, and as the wool is cut draw the strands together and tie in a single knot. When the wool has been cut all round, carefully pull the cardboard rings apart, allowing enough room to wind the strands several times round the middle of the ball. Tie in a firm knot and cut the ends. Now that all the wool is secured in the middle, pull each piece of cardboard away, and you have the woolly ball. If it looks a little shaggy trim away the uneven lengths with the scissors. Bunch it up with the hands and it becomes quite round and fluffy.

A YOUNGSTER'S ALPHABET

Here is something you can easily make which your young brother or sister will appreciate.

Get some rather stiff cardboard and draw on it squares, as shown in the diagram of a cross, letting the side of each square be about 3 inches. Then cut out the cross and lightly score along the lines that divide the figure into squares. Next fold along the scored lines, and so make a

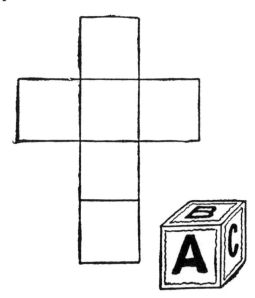

cube. Hold the faces of the cube in position and bind the edges together with adhesive tape or the gummed paper which is used so much to-day for doing up parcels.

Make four of these cubes, all on the same plan.

When the binding strips have dried paint the edges with red ink, and then cut out twenty-four squares of paper, the sides of each being

2¾ inches. On each of these papers boldly print a letter of the alphabet ;
but put I and J on the same sheet and similarly with X and Y.   This is
done to reduce the required number of sheets from twenty-six to twenty-
four. Use various coloured inks for the printing to make it attractive.

Lastly, stick one sheet on each face of the cubes. This toy alphabet
will delight a youngster ; and more, it will help him or her to learn the
letters.

THE ROCKING CAT

Take a piece of stout card, about 14 inches long and 6 inches wide,
and cut it out to approximate the shape shown in the Diagram A.   Make
the slit up the centre barely as wide as the thickness of the card.   Then

A   B

paste paper to cover both the back and front and colour it to resemble
a cat.

Next, cut another piece of card to imitate the shape B, and again, be
careful that the slit is barely as wide as the thickness of the card.   Also,
make quite sure that the distance from the bottom end of the slit to
the foot of this shape is equal to the total length of the slit in shape A.
Paste paper on both faces of this piece of card and colour it to represent
the side views of the lower parts of a cat.

When the two pieces of card have been suitably ornamented, slip
them together, one piece at right angles to the other, the tail at the back
of course, and glue up the slits, so that they will not pull apart.   You
now have a cardboard cat that will stand up and rock sideways, forwards
and backwards in a most fascinating manner.   It will amuse a small
child for hours at a time.

CUDDLY TOYS AND HOW TO MAKE THEM

If you have any very small brothers or sisters there is nothing they would like better than for you to make them a cuddly animal doll which they could hug and punch and pull about to their heart's content. A really attractive creature can be put together in about an hour, and the cost is very small.

Some Cuddly Dolls to Make.

The first thing is to plan your animal. Let it be a simple affair—just a body and four legs—or, simpler still, a wee beastie sitting on its haunches. Your zoo specimen need not be an exact copy of anything in the Natural History museum. In fact, a brightly coloured soft creature of unknown species will give most pleasure.

When you have decided on the form which the cuddlesome thing is to take, cut out two pieces of material to size. Allow for turnings and remember that the animal must have width as well as length and height. The size in the flat must, therefore, be fully large. For the body use Teddy Bear material or plushette. Failing either of these, some odd pieces of velvet will serve. If possible let the legs be in the same piece as the body, so that they will not be liable to come off, and four-legged animals should be given one double leg at the front and another double one behind. Some black stitching run up the middle of these double legs will serve to remind your friends that you have not forgotten that cows and horses are quadrupeds.

Having cut out the material, put the two pieces together, wrong side out, and sew strongly round the legs, head, and hindquarters, leaving but a few inches unsewn along the back. Now turn the thing inside out and stuff first the legs and then the head and body with old stockings and bits of soft flannel. When the creature is bulged out to its fullest limits sew up the opening along the back. It ought now to be a nice soft, plump creature of weird conception.

The trappings remain to be taken in hand. First, the eyes. Above all, do not set them with buttons, as many people do. They are positively dangerous, and may be swallowed. Sew on little ovals of white calico, making the stitches look like eye-lashes. Paint a " gladsome " eyeball on each piece of calico. Add a collar of bright hue, if you desire ; put a black line of stitching for the upturned mouth, and provide a tail, if thought necessary. But do not overdo the frills, and have as few hanging parts as possible, since they will be the first to come off. Aim at something bright, soft, and novel, and remember that children ought not to be surrounded with ugly and frightful playthings. Also, let the cuddly creature be of a size that can easily be held by the particular child for whom you are making it.

FUN AT THE DESSERT TABLE

What a lot of things can be made out of the good fare provided at the dessert table ! There is no doubt that, with a little ingenuity, you will be able to amuse your friends to quite an amazing extent. Look at the pictures. They are all things that you will be able to put together with no great trouble.

No. 1 is a litter of little pigs. The bodies are bananas. Choose those with nice curved sides so that the creatures may appear to have round backs. The ears are shavings cut out of almonds, while the curly tails are little twisted bits of apple. The eyes are slits in the skin, with tiny pieces of apple peel fitted into them. The straw is shreds of apple.

No. 2 is a bunny's head. Select a pear of suitable shape for this model. Provide the ears by curling up two thin slices of apple. Make a hole in which to force them, by using the prong of a fork. The eyes are two tiny sweets embedded in the pear. Cut out a strip of skin to form the mouth. The body-part is half an orange, with a piece cut out to allow the pear to rest on it.

No. 3 is the little ship that was on the sea, mentioned in the well-known nursery rhyme. It is half a walnut. The masts are straight stalks of Muscatel raisins, and the sails are thin slices of apple. Waves, if required, may be formed by cutting wavy strips of apple.

No. 4 is one of those boats which the Romans used. It is nothing more than a suitable banana skin, with dead matches threaded through holes, to serve as oars.

No. 5 is a little chap with a happy nature. His body is formed by cutting the ends from a banana, while his head is a grape. Select one holding on to a stalk. Ram the stalk into the pulp of the banana. The grotesque hands are cut out of almonds, and the round buttons are shaped from some of the pieces left over. The scarf is twisted apple shavings, and the boots are bits of orange peel.

No. 6 is a pugnacious-looking elephant. The head and body are two oranges, fixed by introducing two dead matches into them. Lift up a piece of the peel to make each ear. The tusks are pointed almonds, and the trunk is a curly piece of apple peel. The eyes are small sweets. Stand this creature on banana legs, and spread white sugar around him to hide the cuts.

No. 7 is a racing car. The body is a banana with the ends cut off.

Slice thin pieces off the unwanted ends and use them for wheels. Cut out a place for the driver, and shape the driving wheel out of a slice of banana and a match.

No. 8 is a pair of glasses. Make this out of two empty walnut shells. Pierce a hole in each shell, for the eyes, with a nut-pick or pocket-knife, and make two more slits in each shell for the frame of the glasses. Shape the frame out of spent crackers.

Of course, we have merely suggested eight things that can be made easily. We leave you to originate other little articles from your own imagination.

THE WALNUT TORTOISE

Clever hands can devise all sorts of funny things out of waste material, and our small sisters and brothers love to see us build up playthings out of oddments. Here is one such article. Crack a walnut so that one half of the shell is perfect, and eat the walnut, of course. Now put the

shell, dome side up, on a piece of thin card (a postcard is about the right thickness) and cut out an oval to fit the shell. Leave four projections of card for the legs, and one extra for the head. Run some fish glue round the flat rim of the shell and press the card into contact. When hard and dry, paint the card to match the colour of the shell, bend the legs slightly down and the head up. Thread a length of cotton round the neck and you have a fine little toy which will amuse a youngster for hours. If you make two or three of these walnut tortoises the kiddies will be able to run races with them and have all sorts of fun and sport.

A   USEFUL   NAIL   POLISHER

Take a piece of lint, about 3 inches wide and 4 inches long, and roll it up tightly so that it forms a long, narrow cylinder. Run some strands

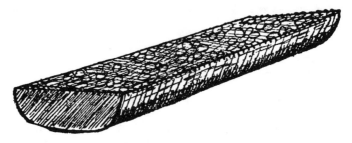

of cotton around it at each end and in the middle, to prevent it uncoiling.

Then obtain a nice smooth piece of chamois leather and roll it round the cylinder, already formed.   Make a few stitches along the line where the leather overlaps.   Fold the ends neatly and stitch them securely.

Now take the cylinder and press it lengthwise, under a warm iron, so that the shape becomes somewhat flattened on two faces with a gentle curve between them.   This should be arranged in such a way that all or most of the stitches come on one of these flattened faces.

The next step is to obtain an attractive piece of silk, brocade or velvet, whichever is at hand, and to sew it over the flattened face where the stitches appear.   The edges must be tucked in carefully and the sewing done as inconspicuously as possible.

You now have a very charming nail polisher for the dressing-table. If one is required for carrying in the handbag, make it in exactly the same way, but considerably smaller.   The lint, then, should make a roll no more than 2 inches long.

A MASSAGE ROLLER

Massage rollers are very popular, and the medical profession claims that by rubbing them along the muscles, there is no better way of keeping yourself fit and trim.   A good roller can be bought for anything between fifteen shillings and two guineas.   You can make an excellent one for half-a-crown.

Go to one of the sixpenny shops in your neighbourhood and buy ten pairs of round rubber heels.   Get five pairs in a medium size and five in a size slightly smaller.   This will give you twenty heels in all.

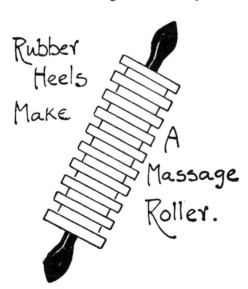

When you reach home, take out any metal parts from the heels and punch a hole through the centre of each, if one is not already there. Then procure a length of curtain rod which will fit in the heel centres. Push the heels on to the stick, large and small ones alternately, as close

v

and tightly together as possible. Then, to both ends of the stick that
are projecting, fit a bicycle handle grip.

It is advisable to begin and end with a large heel. Therefore, use
only nineteen circles and discard one of the smaller heels.

A STRING BOX

String is not ornamental, though it is highly useful. Why not make a
neat little container to hold the ball which mother uses every time she
ties up a parcel ? First, select a clean, empty tin, one that has a round
top, the lid of which presses on. Then take the lid, place it on something
flat, and punch or bore a neat hole through the centre. If the hole you
make is rough, rub it smooth with a file. Now give a coat of
bright-coloured oil paint to the lid and sides of the tin, and when dry add
some ornamental design in oil paints of other colours. Should you feel
rather doubtful about your powers of painting in oils, clean the tin
nicely and cut a sheet of paper to fit the round lid, and another to wrap
round the curved side. Take these and make them gay with a coloured
jazz design, using water colours, and when dry stick them on to the tin
with liquid glue. This will make a nice present for your mother, and it
will be useful, too.

HOW TO GROW LETTUCES

The delicate flavour of a lettuce depends very much on how soon it is
eaten after being taken from the ground. It is clear, therefore, that
home-grown produce has a great advantage over bought specimens.
Fortunately, lettuces are not difficult to grow if the cabbage kind be
selected.

First, a shallow box should be filled with good loam and the seeds sown
about the middle of March. The box should be watered occasionally, and
it is well to move it about to catch whatever sun is available. Also, it
should be screened from boisterous winds and covered up with a sheet
of glass if a late fall of snow comes along.

In late April the best seedlings may be transplanted to their permanent
quarters. When lifting, first water the box, for this will allow the tiny
roots to be got out with a good ball of earth clinging to them. Disturb
these roots as little as possible, and get them into the new ground without
loss of time. As soon as they are in, water them, but do not let the
water fall with such force as to flatten the delicate leaves on to the soil.

This lettuce bed should have been previously manured, and it should
be in a good sunny position. Much water is necessary.

Later on, when other seedlings in the box have grown to a fair size,
transplant them and continue to transplant a few at a time until all
are used up. Those that are pricked out in the summer months should
be put in shady places, such as under trees, or they will never have a
chance of gaining a hold of the ground.

The great thing with lettuces is to have a few reaching maturity at a
time throughout the late spring and summer. If all are transplanted at
the same moment there will be a glut at one period and none at other times.

HOW TO GROW SCARLET RUNNERS

Many people claim that scarlet runners are the most tasty of all vegetables. Whether this is so or not, the average girl will feel a little justifiable pride in providing a supply of her own growing for the table.

Early in May the bed should be prepared. In most gardens the best place will be along a sunny fence or wall. Shady spots are particularly useless. Runners are gross feeders, and they will not grow well unless the ground is given a good dressing of manure. For this, we advise one of the advertised hop manures or, if fowls are kept, some of the sweepings from the runs will do admirably. Whatever manure is used, it should be buried deep down, and not near enough to the surface to come in contact with the early and tender roots.

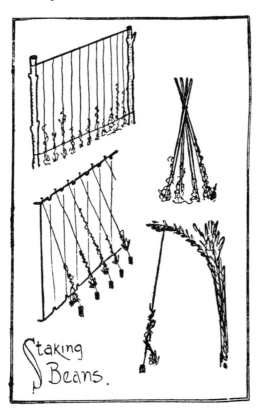

Staking Beans.

Towards the end of May the seed beans should be planted. Push a stick down 2 inches into the ground, drop a bean into the hole, force it to the bottom with the finger, and cover it over. See that the starlings and blackbirds do not dig it up. Place the beans about 8 inches apart. Water plentifully at all stages of growth.

When the young plant begins to throw out its little branches, provide strings for it to climb up. The beans should be ready for picking early in September.

MAKING ICE CREAM

To make ice cream regularly throughout the summer, it is advisable to purchase a proper freezing outfit ; but, if it is only to be made once in a while, it is possible to do with makeshift contrivances. A large, cylindrical tin, placed inside a much larger tin or clean pail will serve quite well. The inner tin contains the cream, whilst the outer one is given, first, a layer of broken chips of ice ; then, the smaller tin is placed centrally on this layer and the sides are packed tightly with alternate layers of ice chips and freezing salt. Use a quarter of a pound of salt to every four pounds of ice. Care must be taken to see that none of the salt runs into the cream. It is advisable to put a tight-fitting lid over the inner tin and to wrap a wet blanket or large towel around the outer tin. In very hot weather, the ice which melts should be run out occasionally, and more ice added to fill the vacant space.

Every few minutes, revolve the inner tin and then cover over the top of the pail with a wet towel. As far as possible, do the work in the coolest spot in the house.

Make the cream in the following manner : Take two eggs, a pint of fresh milk and one ounce of castor sugar. Warm the milk, but do not allow it to boil ; beat the eggs well and stir the hot milk slowly with them ; then add the sugar. Pour the mixture into a double saucepan and stir it over the fire until it thickens, but do not allow it to boil or it will curdle.

If this custard is a little lumpy, when it has thickened, it must be strained before being frozen. The addition of a tablespoonful of cream to this custard, before it is frozen adds greatly to the flavour. Allow the mixture to cool down before putting it into the freezing chamber.

The above recipe provides an excellent ice-cream, but if a special flavour is required, one of the following is advised :

Chocolate Ice Cream.—1 pint of custard (made with eggs, sugar and fresh milk), 4 ozs. of chocolate, $\frac{1}{2}$ teacupful of milk, $\frac{1}{4}$ lb. castor sugar.

Prepare the custard and allow it to cool. Grate the chocolate and stir it into the milk ; add the sugar. Mix well together, then add the custard. Freeze.

Fruit Ice Cream.—1 pint of custard (as above), 1 gill of fresh cream, 4 ozs. crystallized fruit.

Mix the cream with custard (cool), and add the fruit, cut up very small. Freeze, and when firm, serve on a large dish with whipped cream.

Strawberry Ice Cream.—Fresh strawberries, sugar, cream, cochineal or carmine.

Press the strawberries through a sieve. To each pint of purée add $\frac{1}{4}$ lb. of castor sugar and $\frac{1}{2}$ pint cream. Mix well, and add a few drops of cochineal or carmine. Partly freeze the mixture, then whip stiffly another pint of cream, and add it to the freezing cream. Continue freezing till quite firm.

Vanilla Ice Cream.—$\frac{1}{2}$ pint of custard (as above), $\frac{1}{2}$ pint cream, vanilla essence, sugar.

Whip the cream stiffly and add it to the prepared custard after it has cooled. Stir in the vanilla essence and a little sugar, then freeze,

This mixture may be used as a foundation for many different ices variety being obtained by adding fruit juices, flavourings, jams, etc.

SHERBET POWDER

On a hot day, sherbet is an excellent drink. Make the powder in the following way. Mix together

Tartaric acid, 8 ozs.
Carbonate of soda, 4 ozs.
Fine white sugar, 8 ozs.

Store in a dry tin, with a lid that shuts down tightly. Use a teaspoonful of the powder to a glass of cold water.

Although the above is an excellent drink, some people prefer a stronger flavour. For them, it will be advisable to spread out the sugar on a plate or dish, to sprinkle on it thirty to fifty drops of essence of lemon and to dry the sugar in a slow oven. When dry, crumble the sugar, if it has caked, and mix it with the other ingredients, as suggested above.

Of course, any other flavouring essence may be used instead of the lemon, if it is preferred.

COFFEE BRAZILS

Mix a ¼ lb. of ground almonds with the same weight of icing sugar and enough coffee essence to make the mixture the desired colour. Add 1 oz. of butter and work all together until a smooth paste is formed.

Make a syrup of ¼ lb. of loaf sugar and one tablespoonful of water and boil for five to ten minutes. If the almond paste happens to be too thick, moisten it with a very little of the sugar syrup and mix well.

Have ready some shelled brazils. Cover them separately with the almond paste and press them into compact shapes, then, pick them up, one at a time, on the point of a knitting needle, and dip them into the boiling syrup. Let the superfluous syrup drop off, then put on a sieve to drain.

These sweets may be flavoured with melted chocolate instead of coffee essence, if this is preferred.

CHOCOLATE FUDGE

Chocolate fudge is a very popular sweet and it is not difficult to make. This is the way :

Make a mixture of 1 dessertspoonful of chocolate powder, 2 cupfuls of castor sugar, 1 oz. of butter, ¾ of a cupful of milk and a few drops of vanilla essence. Boil this until it will just set, when a few drops are poured on to cold water. Then, remove it from the fire and beat with a wooden spoon until it is nearly cold. It should then be in a creamy condition.

The next step is to pour the material on to a buttered plate or tin and allow it to set. It is then ready to be cut or broken up and eaten.

Remember to do the beating very thoroughly.

COCOANUT ICE

Boil 1 lb. loaf sugar with ½ a cupful of water for about 10 minutes; add 6 ozs. desiccated cocoanut and a little vanilla flavouring and boil again for about 10 minutes; when it has thickened pour half into a tin; keep the remainder in the saucepan hot by standing it in a bowl of hot water, and when the contents of the tin have set, add a few drops of cochineal to that which is in the saucepan and put on top of the white in the tin. When set and cold, turn out and cut into bars.

EVERTON TOFFEE

Put 4 ozs. butter in a saucepan and warm till the butter has melted and covered the pan, then add ½ lb. treacle and ½ lb. moist sugar, stir slowly with a wooden spoon until it boils. Let it boil for about 10 minutes, then test by dropping a little off the spoon in some cold water; if it is crisp it is boiled enough. Butter a large dish or tin, pour the toffee in to cool and leave until set.

CHOCOLATE NOUGAT

Blanch ¼ lb. sweet almonds and cut them in thin slices; mix them with ½ lb. icing sugar; add the whites of two eggs, well beaten, a little vanilla essence, and 2 ozs. melted chocolate, mix with a wooden spoon till it becomes a firm paste. Turn it out on to a tin covered with wafer paper, making it about an inch thick, press it with a knife dipped in boiling water to smooth it and cover with another sheet of wafer paper. Let it dry gradually in a warm place, and when set cut in bars.

PEPPERMINT CREAMS

Roll ½ lb. icing sugar till free from lumps; whip the white of 1 egg and add to the sugar with about ½ teaspoonful of peppermint essence. Mix to a stiff paste; if too dry to work add ½ teaspoonful of water and 1 teaspoonful of cream, if preferred. Roll out on a board sprinkled with icing sugar, to about ½ an inch thick, cut out in rounds with an egg cup or pastry cutter. Allow to stand on a sugared dish for about 6 hours. No cooking is required.

RATAFIA DROPS

Blanch and beat in a mortar 4 ozs. bitter and 2 ozs. sweet almonds with a little of a pound of castor sugar ; then add the remainder of the sugar, and the beaten whites of two eggs, making a paste ; make it into little balls, the size of a nutmeg, lay on wafer paper, and bake gently on greased tins.

MARZIPAN

Boil ½ lb. loaf sugar and ¼ a gill of water for ten minutes ; stir in ½ lb. ground almonds, and cook for five minutes. Remove from the fire, and when cooled mix in the unbeaten white of 1 egg. Replace on fire and cook till the mixture thickens and can be stirred cleanly away from the sides of the saucepan. Turn on to a buttered marble slab and knead until perfectly smooth. Colour and flavour to taste.

BARLEY SUGAR

Boil 1 lb. loaf sugar in a teacupful of water over a slow fire for about half an hour, and keep skimming it as often as any scum rises to the surface. Add a few drops of saffron-yellow, flavour to taste with lemon essence, and turn on to a marble slab. When cool, cut into narrow strips, twist them into spirals, and when quite cold store in air-tight bottles or tins.

CANDIED GINGER

Boil 3 lb. raw sugar in a pint of water till you see the sugar candy round the side of the vessel, then grate some ginger into it, stir it well, and pour out immediately, either into little tin moulds, buttered, or on to a large piece of buttered paper, lay this in a large tin, and pour the ginger sugar on to the paper ; when it cools it may be cut into whatever shapes may be desired with a knife.

CARAMELS

Boil 1 lb. loaf sugar and 1 gill of water, add 1 oz. butter and a pinch of cream of tartar, and stir well ; boil it till it cracks when dropped into cold water, add whatever flavouring is desired, pour into a well-buttered tin to set, and before it is quite cold, cut into squares and wrap separately in grease-proof paper.

LEMON SYRUP

Take a large jar, and put into it 3 lbs. loaf sugar, and pour on it 4 pints of freshly boiled water. Take 4 or 5 lemons, peel off the rind as thinly as possible and add it to the sugar and water. Dissolve 4 ozs. citric acid in a small quantity of hot water, and pour it to the rest. Squeeze the juice from the lemons, strain it and add it to the other liquid. Strain the whole, and bottle and cork closely.

LEMONADE LIQUEUR

Take 6 lemons, grate them against lumps of sugar, put the sugar in a large basin and the juice of the lemons with it and add gradually 4 pints of water ; allow to stand till the sugar is melted, then strain and bottle.

PINEAPPLE LEMONADE

Take a tinned pineapple and grate it into shreds. Place ½ lb. of loaf or lump sugar in a pint of water, or the liquor out of the tin, and boil for five or ten minutes. Then pour it into the vessel containing the grated pineapple, and leave for twenty-four hours. Next, squeeze out the juice from three lemons, put it with the pineapple, and strain out the fragments and shreds. Add water and ice to make four pints of beverage, and serve.

Glossary

alms bag: a bag in which church collections are taken, equivalent to the collection plate

American cloth: a flexible enamelled waterproof cloth resembling leather

beech-mast: a nut, the fruit of the beech tree

butter muslin: a thin, fine-meshed, loosely woven cloth, similar to cheesecloth

calico: closely woven, cheap cotton cloth

card: stiff paper or thin pasteboard

cartridge paper: a strong paper, used for making cartridges in the days of the flintlock, later used for rough drawings

casement cloth: cloth fabric, usually of lustrous finish, used for curtains

castor sugar: granulated sugar

cellulose paint: a paint composed of acetate or nitrate of cellulose, shiny and fast-drying

clothes-horse: a frame on which clothes are hung for drying or airing

copal varnish: a varnish made from a fragrant gum-resin exuded by certain tropical trees

cotton, reel of: a spool of sewing thread; cotton is often used in this book to mean thread

cretonne: a strong, unglazed cloth, usually made of cotton

doyley: a small ornamental mat, made of paper, cotton or linen (var. sp.)

fish glue: glue made from the bladders and other parts of fish

glass-paper: paper covered with pulverized glass, an early form of what is now called sandpaper, used for smoothing wood

gold leaf: gold beaten very thin, used for decorative application

gold size: a sizing material used as a base for the application of gold leaf

greaseproof paper: waxed paper, formerly sometimes called butter paper, because of its primary use, wrapping butter

gum arabic: a specific type of gum derived from several species of the genus *Acacia*

gum: a vegetable secretion from certain trees and shrubs, used on paper or fabrics as a stiffener, mucilage or glue

holland: a linen fabric; when unbleached, called brown holland

huckaback: a stout linen fabric with the weft threads raised alternately so as to form a rough surface suitable for towelling

lint: fine fluff composed of flax, cotton or other fibres, used as tinder, padding or dressing of wounds

lumber room: a storeroom for disused articles

lumber: disused articles, barely worth keeping, not quite ready to be discarded; junk; in this book it does not mean wood

mastic varnish: a fine varnish used for varnishing pictures, made from the resin exuded from the mastic tree

millboard: a stout, coarse pasteboard

mould: loose or friable earth, suitable for gardening

pea stick: a thin stake or stick upon which a garden pea-plant is trained

plushette: a cheaper and inferior type of plush

pochette: a handbag

reel: a spool

sealing wax: a composition of shellac, resins and turpentine, readily melted, that sets to a hard, glossy finish on cooling

shaving papers: squares of paper used for wiping the soap and whiskers from a straight razor during the course of a shave and at its completion

smelling salts: a combination of chemicals possessing a sharp and acrid odour, sometimes combined with oils of more pleasant smell, used as a stimulant to prevent fainting or revive one who has fainted

spirit varnish: a varnish prepared by dissolving resin in alcohol (spirit)

stove black: a black material used for polishing stoves

three-ply (wood): wood consisting of three layers, with the grain of the centre layer at right angles to the grain of the others; an early form of plywood

wadding: a loose fibrous material used as padding; cotton batting

washing soda: sodium carbonate (Na_2CO_3)

watch glass: a shallow glass dish; the protective cover for the face of a pocket watch

xylonite: an early form of plastic, also known as celluloid